Further Praise For Collecting China

"From his base as a solicitor in Hong Kong, Brian McElney travelled very widely in the Far East over the years, unearthing remarkable treasures from the past as he went. The stories of his discoveries, often made in very unlikely corners but always with the unerring eye of the expert, fill this highly readable autobiography. It is a well-rounded tale of applied expertise together with an account of family life and of life as a legal luminary in the Courts of Hong Kong."

—Sir Michael Armitage, former UK Chief of Defence Intelligence

"Brian McElney has given us an account of his life, the core of which has been his work as a prominent lawyer in Hong Kong during its phenomenal economic growth since the mid-1950s, and as a passionate and increasingly knowledgeable collector of Chinese works of art. His journeys, all over the world but particularly in the East, during which he always had his eye open for a possible purchase, make his book a positive travelogue. His commentaries on the characters whom he met or acted for in Hong Kong are fascinating pieces of social history at a time of fundamental change. What an extraordinary phenomenon Hong Kong has been during the span of his career. His legacy is the Museum of East Asian Art in Bath, opened in 1993, which now contains most of his collections and on which, since his retirement, he has lavished his energetic attention."

- Sir Nicholas Goodison, Chairman, National Art Collections Fund (The Art Fund)

"An insider's recollections of the explosive growth of Hong Kong in the latter half of the twentieth century and the opportunities this presented to an avid collector of Chinese art. Fellow collectors will recognise, and appreciate, the 'remorseless persistence' with which he pursued these opportunities and the remarkable collection which resulted."

- *Alan White, CMG, OBE*

COLLECTING CHINA

The Memoirs of a Hong Kong Art Addict

Brian McElney

Collecting China

By Brian McElney

ISBN-13: 978-988-8843-44-2

© 2017 Brian McElney

This book has been reset in 10pt Book Antiqua. Spellings and punctuations are left as in the original edition.

ANTIQUES & COLLECTIBLES / General

EB089

All rights reserved. No part of this book may be reproduced in material form, by any means, whether graphic, electronic, mechanical or other, including photocopying or information storage, in whole or in part. May not be used to prepare other publications without written permission from the publisher except in the case of brief quotations embodied in critical articles or reviews. For information contact info@earnshawbooks.com

Published by Earnshaw Books Ltd. (Hong Kong)

Contents

Foreword	ix
1. Hidden Treasures	1
2. My Family And Assorted Animals	14
3. Mists And Mellow Fruitfulness	35
4. Picnics And Pictures	53
5. Bedsit Land	68
6. In At The Deep End	80
7. Cat Street And Hollywood Road	98
8. Kwai Lo	111
9. Spin The Wheel	127
10. Snapshots Of Hong Kong	140
11. All Change	160
12. Behind The Scenes At The Museum	183
13. A Collector's Treasures	196
Old China Hand	207
My Life In Twenty-Five Objects	215
Acknowledgements	223
Appendices	225

Foreword

by Colin Sheaf

IT IS A TRUTH UNIVERSALLY acknowledged, especially in the upper reaches of the art world, that a great collection is more than the sum of its constituent objects. The collector's own personality is reflected in the composition of the collection; his priorities, his preoccupations, his knowledge. And the collection also reflects the historical and cultural context in which it was formed; the availability of certain items, offered for sale possibly for the first and last time; the contributions of scholars, providing new research which illuminates (and sometimes reconfigures) the academic landscape; and perhaps a new public interest in a particular moment of cultural history, as a spotlight unexpectedly settles on it. A significant collection is not simply a grouping of autonomous objects, brought together on an expensive whim. A noteworthy collection is a time capsule, sealed at a particular moment of art availability (often only transitory), and a window into the collector's own character.

Painstakingly assembled over many years travelling around South East Asia, while he practised as an eminent solicitor in Hong Kong, Brian McElney's collection of Chinese art is a particularly clear demonstration of the 'universal truth'. Many Chinese and South-East Asian ceramics came onto the market from discoveries in the Philippines, Thailand and Indonesia in the 1960s and early 1970s, and by the mid-60s the best of the

COLLECTING CHINA

Hong Kong dealers were bringing many of their finds back to Hong Kong to fuel that emerging market. Therefore the specific circumstances of buying Chinese art throughout Asia, in Brian's case from the 1960s onwards, presented great opportunities to a committed collector with a passion for the mainland's historical artefacts, during the years when China was undergoing and emerging from the shocking brutality of the Cultural Revolution. The art-dealing communities which he visited in Japan (notably in Tokyo and Kyoto), Taiwan, Hong Kong, Singapore, Thailand, Indonesia and the Philippines often favoured collectors with a preference for challenging, unusual and scholarly objects, rather than for blander market favourites or 'blue chips'. It benefitted those willing to learn from, and share knowledge with, the wide range of Chinese and Western academic experts, who visited fast-emerging Asia with increasing frequency, as the cultural environment expanded during these decades in response to greater prosperity and more tourists.

Like a few other professionals around him, Brian merged the analytical mind of a lawyer with a restless urge to learn more about new aspects of early Chinese civilisation as they began to unfold in front of him. Blessed (or cursed!) with the remorseless persistence of a collector who could not conceive of a collection as being complete, Brian McElney occupies a unique position in Hong Kong's pantheon of distinguished collectors of Chinese art.

It was not difficult to become a collector in Hong Kong during the 1970s. Initially Upper Lascar Row and Cat Street, and latterly Hollywood Road (when Government impetus led to much of it being redeveloped as brick properties), were legendary Meccas for Asian and Occidental collectors and dealers. Every day, the serried ranks of cluttered dusty shops and transient stalls (sometimes merely an old mat on the pavement, littered with

BRIAN MCELNEY

bric-a-brac) offered to eagle-eyed buyers the opportunity to pick through very occasionally the world's finest, and most often the world's most mundane, Chinese art; the flotsam and jetsam of one of the world's longest and most distinguished cultures, grievously disrupted by fifty years of domestic, economic and political chaos. Fueled by a continuous supply of art from around Asia, particularly during the 1980s and 1990s, the committed collector could pick and choose amongst a galaxy of artefacts (not for nothing did one of the most prolific dealers call his shop 'Galaxie Art'). Moreover, the best local dealers had almost all become outward-looking, with some now regularly travelling to the major Western auction and retail centres of Chinese art (especially London and New York) to bring back to Asia those fine Chinese objects long buried in Occidental collections. Indeed, the Museum Collection contains items sourced as far afield as Melbourne, Florence and Salt Lake City...and of course in London, New York and Paris.

The opportunities were abundant, but careful selection was key. This was where Brian stood out, often buying against the conventional grain. He ventured into sectors where many collectors feared to tread; archaic and early jades, ceramics from uncharted kiln sites (where later excavations would often confirm his hunches as to date and origin), minor crafts like carved bamboo. A walk with Brian, on his traditional Saturday afternoon 'Progress' down Hollywood Road (by now the 'sweet spot' of the whole artefacts trade in Asia), would inevitably throw up a range of opportunities and challenges. A black-glazed tea bowl – certainly Southern Song dynasty, but made in Fujian or Henan? A calcified jade square cylinder – possibly an unpublished example from the Neolithic Liangzhu culture, but is it merely an acid-treated pastiche? A documentary bamboo brush pot intriguingly carved with a cyclical date within China's

60-year cycle – but does the crisp carving of literary figures studying a scroll inside a thatched pavilion suggest the date should be identified as AD 1782, 1842 or 1902? A Han dynasty silver-inlaid bronze belt hook – but has the elaborate inlay been added recently, to enhance a genuine but routine fashion accessory some 2,000 years old? In a street nearly a mile long, offering Chinese art spanning some 7,000 years of continuous creativity, it took (and takes) an immensely disciplined and experienced eye to winnow the wheat from the chaff.

Walking around the cabinets in the public museum of his collection, which Brian has established in Bath, a classic 18th century city in South-West England, it is clear that the winnowing process was thorough, unemotional and prescient. What is left is a collection rooted in the unique circumstances of Chinese-art trading throughout Asia since the 1960s. It is the fruit of one man's remorseless pursuit of the unusual, the documentary and the didactic, from London to Luk Yu, Hong Kong's legendary tearoom where collectors gathered daily. It is a formidable legacy for students of Chinese art. I am delighted to have collaborated with Brian during his Odyssey.

Colin Sheaf
Chairman, Bonhams Asia and United Kingdom
2016

CHAPTER 1
HIDDEN TREASURES

IT WAS 1967, and I had been living in Hong Kong for nearly a decade. Although there had been sporadic outbursts of violence since my arrival, Hong Kong normally was one of the safest cities in the world, a haven of peace and prosperity, a sanctuary of stability, law and order. As such it had attracted many Chinese to cross the border from the mainland: Mao Zedong was reaching the height of his powers and the growing tensions and fears for the future were prompting many Chinese to flee.

But now the problems were following them. The Cultural Revolution had begun just a year earlier and the chaos that ensued was tipping over into the colony. Shocking newspaper reports were alerting the residents of Hong Kong to the fact that the Red Guards were now deliberately destroying many priceless objects of China's cultural past, including Sakya Monastery in Tibet, a library which contained many ancient Buddhist sutras and other texts which I was to visit in 1984. Had it not been for Mao's right-hand man Zhou Enlai, who ordered units of the People's Liberation Army to stop the Red Guards from entering some of the country's museums, even more of that cultural heritage would have been lost. But enough was being destroyed to cause me very grave concern, because although under normal circumstances

COLLECTING CHINA

Hong Kong was one of the safest places in the world, these were not normal circumstances. Violence was beginning to spill across the border and although the ex-pat community in the colony was considered to be very safe, the news of the Red Guards' vandalism touched a raw nerve.

Since my arrival in Hong Kong, I had begun to amass a collection of Chinese art, and although it was still in its infancy, numbering at that stage less than fifty pieces and only a few of those Imperial ones, it would one day become a collection that was both valuable and culturally important. And with Hong Kong up in arms, increasing rumours of a Chinese invasion, riots, demonstrations and the furious response from the British authorities, I was increasingly concerned that the beautiful pieces in my possession might be at risk.

I had been interested in everything, and having been made a partner in my firm a couple of years previously, I was now in a situation where I could pursue my passion for collecting: glazed ceramics still shimmering with all the colours of the rainbow despite the fact they had been created so very many centuries ago, mysterious jades, rare brasses, iridescent ivories, pottery figures, wooden tree sculptures, corals, lacquers – and in those early days, as I began to track down pieces just as the hunter in the jungle goes after its prey, I felt as if I was capturing them. For me, collecting has always been about so many things, and one has certainly been the thrill of the chase. My fifty or so pieces were housed in my apartment and for the first time the horrifying thought occurred to me: if, as had been rumoured, the Chinese marched across the border, would they too be destroyed by the Red Guards?

These beautiful pieces had survived many centuries of tumult as China transformed from an Imperial power to the Communist superstate it had now become, but as the violence on the streets of Kowloon in that long, hot summer intensified, I became seriously concerned that this latest bout of mayhem, against another once mighty Imperial power, might really be too much, although in every other sense we expats felt safe. The violence was very localised and the people who were seriously concerned were the Chinese incomers from the mainland, who already knew what the Communists were like. They had been allowed to leave Shanghai to take up residence in Hong Kong but on the proviso that they could only take what they could carry, and at one stage 25,000 refugees were flooding in monthly to what was a tiny land area (something that might be of interest to people who are worried about the current levels of immigration into the UK). And now the very trouble from which they had escaped seemed to be following them: they were becoming very worried that they might again become the targets of agitators in Hong Kong. Another exodus began, this time of the Hong Kong Chinese heading to Canada to escape, in many cases for the second time, the Communists and in some cases from the starvation that followed on from their disastrous five-year plans.

The trouble was spreading out from the mainland but in some instances localised labour disputes were now building up to clashes between the British establishment and Communists agitating for Chinese rule. In May that year, riot police were called to an artificial flower factory in San Po Kong and as arrests and allegations of police brutality flared, the violence spilled out further on to the streets.

We expat British were not concerned in the way the Chinese were: the areas in which we lived were relatively unscathed and for many of us the troubles were more of a nuisance than anything else. Almost all the agitation was happening in Kowloon, not on Hong Kong Island (with a few major exceptions) and the Central business district was functioning quite normally. But the Chinese who had sought shelter in the colony did not feel safe. Sentiments against the British were running high in some quarters sympathetic to the Communist regime: lefties, as they were known, were trying to harness public opinion, with some of the local media referring to the British authorities' "fascist atrocities". Up in Beijing (or Peking, as it was then known), demonstrators protested outside the British Chargé d'Affaires office.

Could it affect me? On a day-to-day level, no. My flat, which I had bought in 1960 when it was still under construction and moved into four years later, was in Rockymount, a block of apartments on Conduit Road, the highest point of the Mid-Levels area of the Island, and the rioters never got that far up to what was a pleasant residential neighbourhood. It was more of a problem at work, although mainly because the disruption made it difficult to work: I was a partner in Johnson Stokes & Master, a lawyers' firm with a very long-standing presence in Hong Kong, which at the time occupied the fourth floor of the Hong Kong and Shanghai Bank building. Just about ten yards away from the window of my office you could see the balcony of the Bank of China, which had been annexed (briefly) by the demonstrators, who made such a ruckus you could hardly hear yourself think.

Constant chanting and agitation throughout the day just grew in intensity, making it impossible to work. There was not a great deal of concern about our actual personal safety – there were parts of Hong Kong that we knew to avoid and only once was I caught in the middle of severe disruption, when I caught a tram in the Wan Chai district on my way to see an old friend. The tram came to an abrupt halt with no explanation and there was a great deal of commotion as demonstrators chanted their grievances and onlookers milled about, unsure of what was going on. The next day, I discovered that a fake bomb had been planted on another tram, causing chaos across all the tram services on the Island, but there was no sense of personal danger, merely inconvenience. On that particular occasion, I simply got out and walked.

But even if we didn't feel personally under threat, people began to think about arranging their affairs to safeguard their own property and interests, for if China invaded, as many feared they would, there was a real chance that property of all sorts could be confiscated. The Cultural Revolution had called for the destruction of the "Four Olds" – old customs, cultures, habits and ideas – which in practical terms as far as I was concerned meant that Mao Zedong and his thugs were carrying out the wholesale destruction of the type of artefacts that I had spent a decade collecting. My unease over my own modest collection grew.

The violence was intensifying and becoming more sustained as the leftists shouted their pro-communist slogans and formed huge crowds as high as Government House located on the mid-levels on Upper Albert Road. The transport system all but ground to a halt. The British authorities were beside themselves with fury: Government House was the symbol of colonial rule and this direct challenge to their authority served only to stoke an already incendiary situation. They began to play music from the Supreme Court building to drown out the crowd: Beethoven was one great favourite along with other classical composers, the great masterpieces of Western culture played at earsplitting volume to drown out the protests from the East. The Communists responded with their own high volume music from the Bank of China, immediately opposite the Supreme Court building, both of which were within earshot of my office!

A curfew was imposed banning people from being out after 10.30pm and although the leftists defied this, their protests were given pretty short shrift as they were rounded up and put in jail. And there they stayed, under powers granted by an emergency ordinance which had been on the statute books since the Second World War, with the British determined to show that they were in control.

It was as well that they did so because had they shown any sign of weakness at this point, there was a real chance the Chinese might have walked in. Much of the agitation came from within Hong Kong itself, but there was a growing perception that the Communists might seize the opportunity to retake the colony that so many still considered to be their own. Violence began to grow in other quarters: a police post on the border was shelled from the mainland and three policemen were killed, which was widely believed to be an attempt to gauge the British reaction in the run-up to a much bigger attack. In 2003 it emerged that the People's Liberation Commander in charge of the forces on the border wanted to invade and only refrained from doing so after the idea was vetoed by Zhou Enlai, the first Premier of the People's Republic of China and one of the few senior officials to survive the purges of the Cultural Revolution.

The Chinese exodus from Hong Kong was now well underway. We British expats stayed put, however, not least because we knew that if the Chinese did invade (and they would have had to cross twenty-five miles of leased territories before they got to the Island) there was every chance that they would let the expats leave, as they had done in Shanghai.

Summer in Hong Kong is a very hot and steamy affair indeed and as in so many other cultures, a time when violence is prone to intensify. By July, fatalities began. Amid renewed rumours that the People's Republic of China was planning to march across the border, leftists opened fire on the Hong Kong police, killing five, and the British government, headed by the acting Governor Sir Jack Cater, began closing schools, newspapers and organisations that were known to have leftist sympathies. As leftist leaders were detained, their followers retaliated by planting bombs, real and fake, which killed civilians, including two small children.

A growing revulsion at their tactics followed, but that did not stop them from murdering Lam Bun, a popular anti-left radio commentator, who was burned alive in his car.

Many other prominent anti-leftist figures were threatened and by the time the violence calmed down in the autumn, a total of 51 people had been killed, including 11 police, and a further 832 people sustained injuries. The police behaved admirably in the face of all this provocation: the British were as aware as anyone of the rumour of a Chinese invasion and they did not want to do anything incendiary. They instructed the police to treat the demonstrators with as light a touch as possible and somehow the situation, while very precarious, did not spin completely out of control. This was crucial because had they not done so, the Chinese would have had an excuse to invade on the grounds that they were protecting their own people, but matters never actually came to that.

Soon many of the wealthier Hong Kong Chinese started to find further reasons that made it expedient to take some time away from the colony: although this was never officially made public, rumours soon started to circulate to the effect that the Communists were putting pressure on the tycoons to make "donations" to help them fund the cause.

This was almost certainly true and Hong Kong tycoons were known to be doing as much as they could to protect their own interests. Wild stories abounded as to what people were doing to make sure their personal fortunes were safe. With all the unwanted attention of the Communists, the tycoons didn't want to broadcast their presence and there was a very credible story about one businessman who had been abroad when the troubles began. He was said to have flown into Kai Tak Airport, which was then Hong Kong's international airport (and by common consensus one of the most dangerous airports in the world), and been driven by ambulance to Matilda Hospital on the Peak where he stayed for a few days incognito while he settled his affairs. He then took an ambulance back to Kai Tak and flew off again, leaving the Communists none the wiser, until it was deemed safe to come back.

It was all a far cry from my childhood in Rannerdale in the Lake District and although I wasn't too worried about my own safety, my collection of Chinese art was clearly at risk. Interested in art all my life since an enlightened schoolmaster taught me about aesthetics, I had been adding to the collection for some time now, regularly popping into antique shops and spending the weekends scouring the markets of Hong Kong for treasures to add to my Aladdin's cave. Some of it was out on display but much was packed away in boxes and it also represented part of my own material wealth, along with my partnership, my apartment and a share in the cottage at Rannerdale. The partnership and the apartment could not, for obvious reasons, be moved out of Hong Kong but my collection could. That, and the fact that people were beginning to sell up and move out, gave me some initial ideas about what to do.

Very fortuitously, I had some close connections on the other side of the world, in Canada, and it was total coincidence that Canada was also the location of choice for so many of the others who were exiting Hong Kong. I had no desire to leave the colony but I did want to make sure that my collection was going to be safe and fate had already led me to the place of refuge. I never knew my mother: she died just over a year after I was born, and my father, John Harold McElney, did not remarry for many years. That, however, changed when he became close to an old university friend Margaret ("Madge") Molson and married her in 1958, in the process leaving Hong Kong where he too had been living, and relocating to Victoria, the capital of British Colombia, in Canada.

BRIAN MCELNEY

By the time of the 1967 riots, I had visited several times and had started to see them regularly during the six-week summer break that the firm was now allowing us to take from Hong Kong.

In the course of my trips, I had visited the Art Gallery of Greater Victoria, where Madge was a patron, and had made the acquaintance of its director, Colin Graham. One of my father's Hong Kong partners, Dr James William Anderson, had also visited the museum in the past and a few Changsha pieces from his own collection of Chinese art were on display. I wasn't terribly impressed with the selection as I had some better examples – "I could send you better things than that," I told Colin. And so the germ of an idea, one that was to grow into a long-standing relationship, was born. It began to occur to me that this museum might be just the place to send the collection: it would be safe and the museum itself would be able to show the pieces I sent them. I broached the subject with him when I was there that summer: "Would you like me to send to you an assortment of pieces on loan and you could see what you think?" I asked.

Colin clearly was initially a little bemused. He hadn't seen any of my collection and I had no photographs or descriptions for him. But he agreed.

Once back in Hong Kong I began to make arrangements to have the items shipped out. It had been my custom every time I bought a piece to have a padded box made especially to keep it safe, and so the first step in packing it all up had already been taken. I next had a large aluminium trunk made and once it was complete, I packed some of the collection away to send it to its new home – at that stage much of it was the blue and white china that so many collectors of Chinese art begin with – and with a slightly heavy heart had it taken down to the docks. Shipping, at least, was not disrupted by the violence and fairly soon my collection was on its way from one British colony to another British colony, albeit by now independent, on the other side of the world. I was not unduly alarmed at sending it away: I knew the pieces would be well looked-after and there was certainly no rioting to threaten the status quo in Canada. A few grizzly bears getting aggressive, perhaps, but nothing to rival what was going on in Hong Kong.

A few weeks later, the cargo arrived and Colin Graham took charge of the aluminium trunk when it was delivered to the museum. What happened next was to influence the rest of my life. Without having a clue what to expect, he opened the various padded boxes nestling deep in the trunk – and gasped. He later told me he was staggered at the quality of what he was seeing, bowled over by a collection that was far more notable than he had been led to expect. Colin knew right away that what I had sent him was hugely significant and would prove to be a huge bonus for the museum for as long as they had it. One day, this collection would be housed in a museum of its own.

I know that these days there is a certain amount of debate about taking quality pieces out of China and now that their economy is growing so fast and the growth of Chinese millionaires is ubiquitous, many Chinese are now involved in buying their country's beautiful treasures back. But this is not what it was like at the time. The rioting in Hong Kong – the latest in many bouts of civil unrest – came just one year after the Cultural Revolution and the concerted effort to wipe out China's ancient and sophisticated cultural past. It wasn't just a new political system that was in place: Chairman Mao wanted to wipe a clean slate across China and destroy anything that reminded the people of its Imperial past. It is impossible to estimate quite how many pieces were destroyed, gone forever after falling into the clutches of people who didn't understand them, couldn't appreciate them and would have destroyed them in an instant if they had come upon them before collectors like me found them and managed to protect them from the people who were laying China to cultural waste. Collecting was my passion, but at the same time the result of that passion was to save something precious, and for that I am proud.

Sending my collection to Victoria marked a turning point in my life as a collector however, because this was the first time I had shown my purchases to anyone other than friends. Colin was the director of the museum and as such had seen beautiful and desirable objects from all over the world. His reaction to my pieces thus had a hugely beneficial and happy effect on me because it was an affirmation of my own abilities as a collector and whether I had that all-important (and often elusive) "eye". I knew now that a senior figure in the art world thought that I had put together a beautiful collection and this gave me a huge amount of confidence to pursue this hobby, as I suppose one must call it. And I was unusual among collectors because I was interested in everything. Many people confine themselves to just one area – blue and white china, say, or jades or bronzes. But I wanted all of it. Nothing was ever too much.

And one day this collection was going to form the basis of a museum of its own. Nicole Chiang is now the curator of The Museum of East Asian Art in Bath and she tells me that I was one of the last great collectors of Chinese art in Britain.

"What struck me was the ambition for such a comprehensive collection," she says now. "You collected everything. And this is very much a collector's collection because so many of the pieces are small enough to hold in your hand, to savour and examine. And you had an example of just about every period of Chinese art."

But much of that was still to come. Back in 1967, as the rioting continued in Hong Kong, as China's presence across the border continued to be a menace and my collection settled into its new Canadian home, I had no idea I was going to establish such a significant body of pieces. I only knew that the thrill of the chase was getting stronger than ever and that I wanted to get my hands on as much as I could. But I did know that Colin rated me, and that was very encouraging.

But there were to be changes in my life in other ways back then, too. For a start, I wasn't just worried about my collection: I was worried about my own financial security, and so in 1967 I bought the first of a number of properties in British Columbia, the Bellamy Building at 1401 Government Street, Victoria, BC. My plan for quite a long time was that I would retire there, although ultimately the fates were going to take me somewhere else.

The riots finally came to an end in the autumn of 1967. The Chinese didn't invade and life went back to the way it had been before. Many of the Chinese who had left Hong Kong for Canada now returned, especially the younger ones. The Chinese are famous for being inveterate gamblers and the Hong Kong stock market reflects this: now that it was clear that Hong Kong was going to be British for another thirty years, the market started to soar. Until then, only one or two companies a year would float on the stock market. Now everyone was clamouring to do so, which benefitted me both personally as an investor and also as a lawyer, because our firm was called upon to act for many of these companies.

It was not unusual for shares to rise to a premium of 200 percent. The two emotions that drive the stock market anywhere in the world are fear and greed, and the recent fear about Chinese intentions had given way to a lust for what was coming next. Confidence was further fueled by the fact that in 1967 the Portuguese offered to give Macau back to the Chinese but they refused on the grounds that the timing was not right, with Hong Kong taking this to mean there would be another period free of Chinese control.

BRIAN MCELNEY

And so the next period of tumult got under way, except that this time, instead of being fueled by the Communists, it was the turn of the capitalists. And as money washed over Hong Kong, so a construction bonanza began as the colonial villas that were still in evidence when I moved there began to make way for the city of steel and glass we are all so familiar with today. The changes that I saw in Hong Kong were phenomenal, but then so have been so many changes in the century in which I lived. And this is the story of my life and a changing world, a life that began in the Far East but which drew me, with the treasures of the East, finally back to the West to establish a museum based on those self-same treasures I had found in Hong Kong so very many years ago.

CHAPTER 2
My Family And Assorted Animals

I WAS BORN INTO a century of turmoil: when I made my way into the world it was still reeling from the dreadful aftermath of one world war and heading fast into a second one, wars that were to claim both my father's brothers, one lost in each. Ours is a family that has stretched out all over the globe, for I was born in Hong Kong, the city that would come to dominate my life, a city that itself has changed at least as much as the world around it.

I was born on July 10th 1932 into a family of doctors, which would be unremarkable now but was extraordinary for the time as there had been two generations of doctors on my mother's side. My mother, Ariel Ransford Stewart Deacon, was a doctor before she married my father; she studied medicine at Liverpool University, which is where my parents met. That was unusual enough for the late 1920s, but even more surprising was the life of my grandmother, Mary Ariel Stewart.

Mary qualified as a doctor in 1898, one of the first women ever to do so, and after marrying her husband, Thomas Deacon, she moved to the Gold Coast in 1901 (as Ghana was then known), where he had been appointed Postmaster General and she had been appointed medical officer. They were met on arrival by all the native chieftains, who had come to greet these new strangers in their midst. It was the medical officer that they were interested in, not the Postmaster General, but no one had had the foresight to warn them that this important personage was a woman. When they approached the couple, there was some confusion until they realised the terrible truth – at which point they all rushed back inland in horror. But such was Mary's implacable resolve that in the end she won them round. My grandfather, meanwhile, took the opportunity to found a masonic lodge.

My mother - Ariel Ransford Stewart Deacon McElney

Ultimately, Granny Deacon left the Gold Coast in 1906, two years before her husband was invalided out because he had succumbed to blackwater fever, a very nasty complication of malaria, which often results in kidney failure. Granny, meanwhile, went to work in the British Hospital in Bologna, Italy until 1912. At the outbreak of war in 1914 she joined the ICI munitions factory in Widnes, for which she was awarded an MBE in 1918, the first year in which it was awarded. She went on to become the Director of Public Health in Birkenhead with so many degrees and honours that she ended up with 24 letters after her name. I didn't know my grandfather anything like as well, as he was very much overshadowed by Granny and was to die in 1940.

Their only child, Ariel, my mother, after initial schooling in Italy, had been educated at Roedean and decided to follow her mother's example and while studying tropical medicine at Liverpool met my father, John Harold McElney. A very attractive and lively woman who had kept a motorcycle in the hall of the family home near Liverpool, my mother was a flapper and used

COLLECTING CHINA

My father, Jack and his brother Harper (1939)

to wear a string of natural pearls, which she once broke when riding her mechanical steed, although they were later restrung and passed down to the family. She immediately captivated my father, who was always known to everyone as Jack.

My father was a Son of the Manse. He came from Northern Ireland originally, the son of a Presbyterian parson, the Reverend Robert McElney and his wife Mary Elizabeth née Davison. My paternal grandfather was a very distinguished man: he had an MA from Queen's University, Galway, and was a scholar. I once saw a diary entry of his dating from 1884 noting that he had read three plays by Sophocles in one evening in the original Greek. He went on to become a fellow of the Society of Antiquaries of Scotland and a senior figure in the Presbyterian church. His ministry began in Saintfield, where my uncles were born: Robert Gerald, born in 1892, was awarded the MC in the First World War and died just before the end of it, in 1918. He, too, was a doctor – I come from generations of them on both sides of the family – and served as a captain in the Royal Army Medical Corp.

BRIAN MCELNEY

Then there was William Harper Campbell Davison, born in 1900, who died in the Second World War, who had also started to train as a doctor but had to give it up for health reasons when he was thought to have contracted tuberculosis, and after being advised to leave the UK for sunnier climes, made his way to what was then known as Zululand and is now KwaZulu-Natal, where he managed a big sugar plantation. Coincidentally Wendy, the daughter of the plantation owner, married Sir Michael Turner, chairman of the Hong Kong Shanghai Banking Corporation after the war and they later became good friends of my father in Hong Kong.

In between the two brothers there were three sisters, one of whom was to play a central role in my upbringing. In 1901, my grandfather moved to Downpatrick, where my father was born in 1904. However, when he became an adult my grandfather advised him against living in Northern Ireland, saying that the bigotry was so strong it would be better to make a life elsewhere, and he also thought it would be advisable if my father studied somewhere other than his home turf on the grounds that if Ireland ever gained independence, its medical qualifications might not be recognised in the wider world. He had also been a prison visitor and as such had seen the violence and intolerance on both sides of the religious divide. My father duly qualified as a doctor at Edinburgh University, where he was captain of the rugger team.

It was while he was at that university that he made the acquaintance of a Dr Macgown, over from Hong Kong and in Edinburgh to recruit a new assistant for his firm in the Far East. Bearing in mind his own father's advice to make a life outside Ireland, my father replied to his advertisement. Dr Macgown made him an offer of employment, but asked him to get a further qualification before he went out to the colony. And so, after Edinburgh, my father went on to Liverpool to study tropical

COLLECTING CHINA

Robert Gerald McElney (died 1918)

medicine, which is where he met my mother. However, the link to Edinburgh was maintained: my parents became engaged on the top of an Edinburgh tram. They arranged that he would go out to Hong Kong first and that my mother would follow when she too had completed her tropical medicine degree.

My father departed for Hong Kong in 1928, arriving on January 2, 1929 and worked hard to establish his career. The global economy was extremely precarious and in the decade that followed was to suffer from the Great Depression. The feeling among many at the time was that they were fortunate to be employed.

My father initially worked in Dr Macgown's practice as a GP, with a speciality in tropical medicine and much later became a gynaecologist, not least because his patients were largely European or Eurasian and a gynaecologist was what was required. It was agreed that after my parents married, my mother would join him in Hong Kong. The wedding ceremony duly took place in Singapore in 1930 and after a honeymoon in Sumatra, they settled into their life in Hong Kong, where my father was to spend the rest of his working life, although there was a break for the duration of the Second World War. They first lived in a flat at No. 80 Nathan Road, a large, tree-lined boulevard in Kowloon, before moving to the house in which I was to spend my early years. In those early days, Dr James William Anderson and Dr Durran had already joined the practice as assistants, my father was the third and after him came Dr Dawson-Grove, very much the junior of the quartet.

It was to become a very successful practice. Dr Macgown retired in the mid-1930s and my father and the other assistants acquired the practice in various shares, according to their seniority. After the war, Drs Durran and Dawson-Grove chose not to return, and the firm was renamed Anderson Partners. There had originally been plans to name it after my father until someone pointed out that the Chinese phonetic of his name translated as 'dysentery mac', which would not have been ideal for a medical practice. Dr Anderson himself was still around, but he had been a PoW under the Japanese and had been forced to act as surgeon in the Japanese military hospital. Consequently his health, both mental and physical, had become fragile, so it was my father who got the firm up and running again, going on to employ about thirty doctors. But that still lay ahead.

Very unusually for a European woman at that time, my mother also worked: she was an employee of the Hong Kong government at Queen Mary Hospital where she worked for the sum of HK$6,250 a year. (At that stage the exchange rate was fluctuating wildly with the price of silver, from ninepence up to five shillings, before stabilising in the mid-1930s with one Hong Kong dollar the equivalent of about one shilling and thrupence).

The family still has a long letter from 1930 which she sent to her mother, describing her new life in Hong Kong and containing numerous photographs, one of which was of a sow and piglets with the caption, "I've even seen a sow and piglets crossing the road in front of the tram on Hong Kong Island." It almost certainly happened in Shaukiwan, which was in those days a little fishing village at the end of the tram line. Like everything else, it has totally changed and now contains a six-lane highway and a tram line going up the centre, with buildings of up to forty storeys on either side.

The letter, which to the modern eye reads almost as a travelogue, was written to fill my grandmother in on a lifestyle totally different from that back in the UK. It starts with a detailed handwritten map of the Island, and takes the reader on a written journey, complete with photographs, which would have been professional postcards. It is divided into sections, covering Kowloon to Hong Kong, The Harbour, and Hong Kong City and there are numerous captions to chart what is going on.

BRIAN MCELNEY

Beside the picture of the harbour, my mother commented that it was the third best in the world after Rio and Sydney. Alongside a picture of the most common form of transport at the time, she wrote, "There are always plenty of rickshaws, so you just shout 'sha' and they come running up seeing who can get there first". There are snapshots of Chinese life: a group of amahs having a chat; Aberdeen fishing village with a seagoing junk in the foreground and a sampan behind, and a shot of Chinese streets in Kowloon with an arrow pointing to the location of "Jack's tailor." Perhaps the most exotic shot to Western sensibilities was the outside of a joss house: this, my mother explained, was where the Chinese went to throw joss sticks to know what their fortune would be.

I arrived two years later, and was christened Brian Shane McElney after delivery at St Paul's hospital in Causeway Bay, which my father always referred to as the French hospital as it was staffed by French nuns. The following year my mother fell pregnant with my brother Desmond Harper and returned to Liverpool to have the baby, which is when tragedy struck. Desmond was born on August 13th, but my mother contracted blood poisoning, something that these days would be easily cured with a dose of penicillin, but in 1933 it was not available.

My father was informed and set out immediately from Hong Kong with me in tow, while under the agonised eyes of her family – so many doctors and unable to save her – her illness became much worse. She continued to deteriorate until the outcome was clearly going to be a tragic one, and on October 13th that year she died, exactly two months after her second child was born. She was only 29, the same age as my father, who was devastated, all the more so he as reached Liverpool only a few days after she had died. Granny had also lost her only child. Granny was a formidable woman, the type spoken of as being found in outposts all over the Empire, but she was so badly shaken that for a while she was quite unable to cope. We stayed on for several months while the family decided what we should do next: my father would return to Hong Kong with now two very young sons but how would he manage? The custom at that time in Hong Kong was to work for four years and then take one year's leave, which is how he was able to take so much time off at this point.

And so I met one of the dominant figures of my childhood, Aunty Mary. Mary Caroline Wilkinson, who was born in 1896, was one of my father's older sisters and, again unusually for the time, was divorced. When it was time for us to return to Hong Kong she decided to accompany us to keep an eye on my father and make sure we children were going to be all right. Aunty Mary was a typical product of her times: punctilious in speech with a list of forbidden vocabulary (we were never, ever allowed to say, "What?") and a marked manner when speaking on the telephone, so typical of the women of her day; she cut a trim and proper figure that belied a real independence of spirit.

And so for now, it suited brother and sister that she accompany our father back. This was a different time: a widower, especially one with very small children, was not expected to look after them himself and various family members rallied round both then and throughout the rest of my childhood to help. "Daddy was propping up the bar on the way back while Aunty Mary looked after us," was how my brother put it wryly many years later of the boat journey back to Hong Kong.

Aunty Mary had a daughter who was three years older than me, Anne Mary Diana Wilkinson, (now Fraser), and once back in Hong Kong we all lived in the same house. With a shock of golden curls, Anne could have been another Shirley Temple; as it was, she was more like a sister to me than a cousin, sharing our lives until 1937 when they returned to England. Divorce was very uncommon back then but on her own, and without many

BRIAN MCELNEY

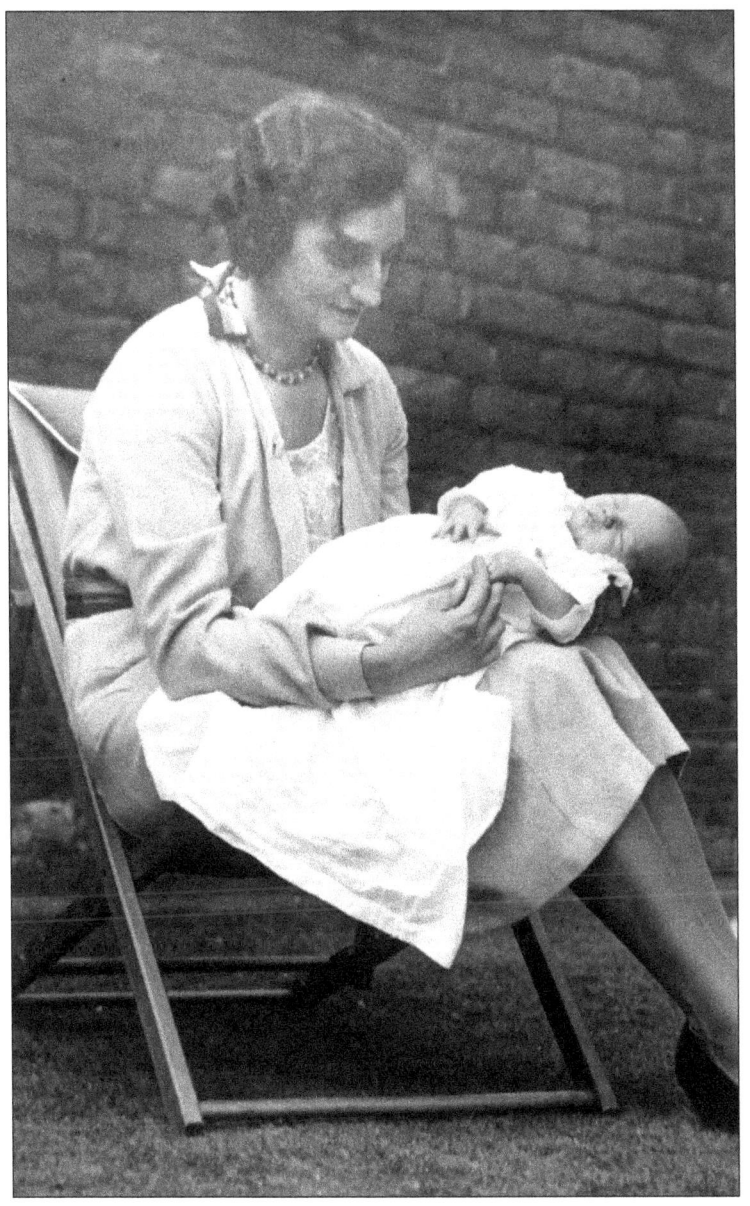

Ariel and Desmond

resources, Mary managed to give my cousin Anne a happy and fruitful childhood.

Under Aunty Mary's supervision, we were looked after by a succession of Chinese amahs, wearing their trademark black trousers and white cotton shirts. Hong Kong was a very different place back then from the city I was to know as an adult: for a start, there were far fewer people, only about one and a half million. The common form of transport was the rickshaw and the only way to cross Victoria Harbour was by ferry. Victoria Harbour itself was a fascinating place for a child, filled with sampans, junks, ferries, freighters, cargo ships, ocean liners, yachts and warships. It was the seventh-busiest harbour in the world, and crucial to Hong Kong's development as a major trading centre. As an adult, I was to buy an apartment that overlooked it and watched it transform into the focal point of modern Hong Kong.

British rule had been well established with Britain taking a 99-year lease on the New Territories and outlying islands in 1898. Hong Kong Island itself had been granted in perpetuity after the first Opium War in 1843. The very well-off British lived in large colonial mansions, tended to by Chinese servants including houseboys and drivers, who wore uniforms; most of the rest of us were comfortable, even if not living in such lavish style. By now we resided in Gomez Villas at No. 1 Chatham Road in Kowloon, in a house that no longer exists, a typical colonial villa, although it was backed right up against Observatory Hill with no back garden; only some outside space at the front. My father's life was mainly devoted to work, but when he did entertain, his guests included both expats and the more prominent Chinese and Eurasian families, which was not at all the norm at the time. Members of Eurasian families were often known by both European and Chinese names and one of them, Wilfred Tyson/Chan, was to become a lifelong friend.

BRIAN MCELNEY

Me, Granny Deacon and Desmond (1934)

Wilfred's father Kenneth Chan (or Kenneth Tyson) went on to marry Jessie Wong (also known as Jasmine), one of the first-ever Chinese women to attend the University of Cambridge. They in turn had Wilfred Chan, who went on to become one of my closest friends, in later years helping his mother to run the family's wine and spirits company, Gande Price & Co. Indeed, I was extremely close to the whole family. One of my earliest recollections, although I can remember no details given that I was about three at the time, was attending Wilfred's third birthday party which, suitably for someone of such a background, was held at the Peninsula Hotel. At that point the Peninsula was the best hotel in the Far East and its reputation is still supreme. No expense would have been spared despite the youth of the birthday boy and to this day, Wilfred still has the silver tray on which the drinks were served.

That party was a great success but the same could not be said for every entertainment that was laid on back then. I attended another party after which about twenty of us guests, all children, contracted bacillary dysentery, probably from infected milk, and although my father was able to treat Desmond and me, some of the children died. Life could be cheap back then. On another occasion my father and friends were travelling by car back from Fanling in the New Territories on the terribly narrow little tree-lined roads. Quite suddenly and unexpectedly, an elderly lady appeared out of nowhere from behind one of the trees and stepped in front of the car, which screeched to an abrupt halt, but it was too late. It was almost certainly a suicide, because life was quite desperate for the poverty-stricken back then, and the woman's actions appeared entirely deliberate.

My father leaped out of the car and tried to revive her, but to no avail – she was already dead. Her family appeared from across the fields and after they had established what had happened, my father and his friends gave them HK$100 (about £20 at the time) and prepared to leave. The farmer asked the party to wait as there were other elderly relatives who were prepared to jump in front of a car – a measure of the desperation of some parts of the local community, which had been pushed into dreadful straights by the effects on the colony of the 1929 Wall Street crash – HK$100 would have been enough to buy two paddy fields at the time. Of course, they did no such thing and drove off.

My father's work as a doctor did sometimes put him in an awkward position as on another occasion he was called out to tend to a man who had had a heart attack. My father arrived at the family's home at about 9.30am, and again found there was nothing he could do as the man was already dead. The family tried to get him to register the time of death as 11am and although my father did not go along with their request, there was a perfectly good reason behind it. The widow wanted to be able to get to the bank and empty the family's safe deposit box before her husband was officially declared dead because as soon as a death occurred, deposit boxes were sealed and would only be opened after an inventory of their contents had been witnessed by someone from the Estate duty office, and death duties could range up to 52 percent, an amount that was deeply resented by the local community and which many did their best to avoid.

However, there were also lighter moments. My father had loved rugby at Edinburgh and that passion had never faded, and so in the 1930s he instigated a local seven-a-side tournament in Hong Kong. This went on to become the Blarney Stone 7 (the other players were also of Irish origin) and became a fixture on the Hong Kong circuit throughout the twentieth century.

There was plenty to intrigue my younger brother Desmond, Anne and myself. For a start we lived next door to a family called Loseby. He was a lawyer, but what was far more exciting for Desmond and me was that she was the head of the Hong Kong RSPCA and the family had three baby pandas in their front garden along with a Malayan honey bear, who was in fact going to stay in my life for some time. My childhood was to be filled with animals of various descriptions and these pandas were the first.

When I was older I learned, however, that Mr Loseby had a life that was quite as interesting as that of his wife. In 1930, a couple of years before I was born, a Vietnamese agitator by the name of Nguyen Ai Quoc had visited Hong Kong and while he was there – in fact, while he was at the Loseby's house – he had founded the Communist Party of Vietnam. Quoc was later to be known as Ho Chi Minh, the first President and Prime Minister of the Democratic Republic of Vietnam, and even then he was causing trouble, with the French issuing a warrant for his extradition. Loseby successfully defended him on the grounds that a political extradition, which this would have been, was illegal. Eager to resist the pressure from the French, the British authorities then falsely allowed it to be known that Quoc had died before quietly releasing him from incarceration. In later years, the Losebys were invited to visit Vietnam, where they were treated like royalty (or as royalty would have been treated were Vietnam not a Communist state). As an adult I, too, travelled to Vietnam, where I discovered that Loseby featured in the Ho Chi Minh Museum – where he was incorrectly described as Lawyer Lose.

But how could future Communist dictators compare to pandas for two little boys? I was sent to a nursery school, of which I have no recollection, but I do remember going about on boats and going to the beaches to go swimming. One of the beaches had matsheds – huts made out of bamboo mats and raised several feet from the ground. We frequently took Granny's cockatoo with us, which would trot along the beach after us, another of the numerous animals that were to make a mark on my childhood.

We were there during times of great excitement, but also tragedy, for we were there during the Great Typhoon of 1937, which took place overnight on September 2nd. It remains to this day the worst typhoon in Hong Kong since the colony was founded in 1843, killing 11,000 people. Forecasters were only able to give twenty-four hours' notice of the catastrophe that was on its way, and by the time the storm hit, winds were up to 150 miles per hour. There were observatory instruments that were supposed to be capable of registering winds of up to 125 miles per hour which broke down, unable to cope. Victoria Harbour, full of all that shipping, was devastated – up to 20,000 tonnes of shipping was lifted up and smashed on to the rocks, a tidal wave swamped Tai Po and Sha Tin and killed thousands. Fish were swept up out of the harbour and were later found on the roofs of buildings that were over fifty metres high.

We were terrified. The winds hit our house with unbelievable force, so strong it seemed the windows would be blown out of their frames and we were right to be so. Desmond and I shared a bedroom at the front of the house and during the night made our

BRIAN MCELNEY

Anne (standing), Desmond, Aunt Mary and me (Hong Kong 1937)

way towards the back, where my father slept, and very fortunate it was that we did. The windows at the front of the house finally blew in and the ceiling came down, and we could have been badly hurt if we'd stayed there. Not that the back was inviolate: that was where the kitchen was and a huge rock came flying through the air and smashed into it. The house was something of a wreck and for what was to turn out to be our last months in Hong Kong, we had to move again, this time to 288 Prince Edward Road.

But we were the lucky ones. The typhoon made headlines all over the world, with many eyewitness accounts of the terrible extent of the damage, with reports of the harbour and its smashed-up boats, collapsed buildings, fires rampaging and lives and livelihoods lost. The worst of it was at Tai Po and Sha Tin where the tidal wave smashed onshore. It destroyed villages, washing villagers out of their beds and to their deaths, progressing a quarter of a mile inland before it finally came to a stop.

The Observatory Director, CW Jeffries, later prepared a report about what had taken place. "It is doubtful if a storm of greater severity and destructive power has ever visited the Colony," he wrote. "At the height of the storm a tenement block of nine four-storeyed houses in the Western District went afire and 15 inmates perished… Several buildings were unroofed, old houses collapsed, garden walls were blown down, roads blocked by landslides, fallen telegraph poles and uprooted trees. Among the many ships in the harbour were some laid up because of the war, or under repair at docks and without steam. A score of these broke loose from their doubled moorings and careered drunkenly about the harbour in a macabre dance. The Star Ferry pier suffered extensive damage."

By this time, Desmond and I were five and six and with the best will in the world, my father was finding it very difficult to cope with two lively little boys without a wife, not least because

Aunt Mary and Anne had by now returned to England. It began to appear to everyone that it might be better if we were sent back to the United Kingdom too, and to that end my grandmother Mary Deacon, my mother's mother, had come out to stay with us for a few months to take their place and to help prepare us to return home. She was by now retired and travelling with a companion called Miss Hyde, of whom more anon. The time was nearing for us to return to England and my father needed Granny's help.

A sense that change was in the air followed us wherever we went. When Granny Deacon took us out for a picnic in the hills, we got caught up in a hill fire which probably started after someone threw away a lit cigarette, and we had to take shelter in a stream. To us boys, it was an adventure, but could the sight of the New Territories up in flames be a presentiment of the violence that lay ahead?

The thinking was that my father wouldn't come back with us at that point but would visit us on his next leave to the UK. Granny and my father arranged for us to travel on the *SS Sarpedon*, a cargo liner of the Blue Funnel line, which also had the capacity to carry 155 passengers and so the five of us, Granny, a newly-engaged nanny called Miss McKay, Miss Hyde and we two boys boarded the ocean-going giant and set off on our six-week tour back to England, a cold and rainy country that was totally alien to me back then. But our journey was unusual in some respects. Granny absolutely doted on animals and was bringing a few back with us from Hong Kong to join the household – the Malayan honey bear and a wallaby (another rescued animal) from next door (both actually destined for Chester Zoo), the cockatoo (that we took to the beach) and a Macaque monkey called Judy.

As a final party before leaving Hong Kong, we took all our school friends to the première of Disney's new film, Snow White and the Seven Dwarfs.

COLLECTING CHINA

Me and Desmond returning to the UK (1938)

We did not travel light: there were no fewer than thirty-five of our packing cases on the journey back to the UK. As on many long ship journeys, entertainments were laid on to amuse us. On one occasion, there was a fancy dress party and my brother Desmond attended as Cupid although what I myself appeared as has been lost in the mists of time. On another, having seen some of our fellow passengers fishing, we decided to try our own luck, obtained a line with a hook on it and threw it over the side. It didn't actually extend as far down as the water, but we were unaware of that and so, some minutes later, were greatly excited to feel a tug on the line. When we hauled it up, however, bewilderment turned to hilarity when we realised what had happened – the line had gone past the galley window and some wag had grabbed it and attached a Finnan haddock to the hook. This was intensely amusing to us as children. So we passed the voyage happily, on another occasion cutting one another's hair as a way of passing the time.

In later life, I was to travel extensively and although I wasn't to know it, this turned out to be one of the first of such trips, with a stop to visit another far-flung member of the family, great uncle Thomas Bruce Stewart on my mother's side, who lived in Columbo, the capital of what was then Ceylon and is now Sri Lanka, with his wife Marie. Another of the many members of my family who thrived in various outposts of the British empire, he was an engineer and head of the waterworks and the couple lived in some style with their daughters Pam, Yvonne and Mary. Our ship docked to discharge cargo and we lunched in the beautiful Mount Lavinia hotel. I can just remember being taken to the zoo, where amid some excitement I was taken to ride on an elephant.

And with that, it was back to the ship, scampering around and entertaining ourselves as we continued the journey from the Far East back to northern Europe. The ship docked again in

London to discharge cargo and we briefly disembarked again, wearing horrible little brown velvet suits of the type associated with Little Lord Fauntleroy, which Desmond and I destroyed as we rampaged about the place, where for the first time I met two other relatives who were to play a large part in my life: Aunt Flops (really Florence Agnes, the second of the Rev. Robert McElney's children, born in 1894) and her husband Francis William Davies. And then it was aboard again for the last short stretch of the voyage, and eventually the ship docked in Liverpool. The next stage of my life, my English childhood, began.

CHAPTER 3
MISTS AND MELLOW FRUITFULNESS

WHEN I RETURNED TO England it was a completely new country for me. While I had technically been there briefly when I was about a year old, I was a real child of Empire and I had no recollection of Great Britain. This cold, rainy grey country bore little in common with the steamy exoticism of Hong Kong which was, after all, where I had been born. And this was a new set-up for Desmond and me: my father was still in Hong Kong, Aunty Mary and Anne were living in Great Bedwyn in Wiltshire and I was about to be exposed to the English public school system, something I had never experienced before. Even so, I wasn't homesick: I was with my Granny and my brother, I had some family in the UK to get to know, and I knew my father would be visiting us soon. As it turned out, his first visit to Europe coincided with the outbreak of war and he ended up staying for much longer than had been the original plan.

The world we lived in back then, as Europe lurched horribly and inexorably towards war, has now vanished, as comprehensively as the Hong Kong I knew when I was a child. Granny, who had retired two years earlier, had lived for some years in a big 22-room house with her husband Tom – 22 The Esplanade, in the suburb of Waterloo, about five miles north of the centre of Liverpool and

COLLECTING CHINA

Granny Deacon

five-hundred yards from the docks at Bootle, with a lovely walled garden with a door that opened onto the beach, and a glass conservatory. It was rented from the Mersey Docks and Harbour Board, a large three-storey Victorian house with rooms placed around a central well. But Granny was nothing if not a character and her household reflected her own unusual past. For a start, she had spent all her life practising as a doctor and she clearly felt that retirement shouldn't put a stop to that.

She decided that she would take in people with mental problems, not people who were actually certifiable but those who were, to put it politely, eccentric. Miss Hyde was one of these, and many years later it emerged that she was probably schizophrenic. Granny's nephew Dr Robert Howard Mackenzie Stewart (known to everyone as Mac) later wrote a pamphlet about Granny entitled Buoyancy Of Spirit. In it, he speculated that the reason she decided to run what was in effect an extraordinary household was that Tom didn't have much of a pension and Granny needed to earn something extra if she wanted to continue to live in style. And that she certainly did. Granny spent money like water and the impending war did nothing to stop her, although it should be said that to those around her, she was generous to a fault. Her influence was very beneficial as well: Mac lived there himself for a while, although he had gone by the time we arrived, and he went on to have a very successful career as a doctor, running many of the hospitals in the northeast. This was entirely down to Granny, who had persuaded him to go to medical school.

Miss Hyde herself was an interesting character. Her father, Edwin Hyde, had been a draper and had once employed H.G. Wells as an apprentice. When she lived with Granny, she had two Pekinese called Toto and Mimi and suffered from terrible restlessness, never able to sit down for a minute. She was wealthy, though, having been left a tidy sum by her father, and when the time came for the two of them to visit Hong Kong, while this was explained as being good for Miss Hyde's health, she paid for everything. She was also treated more as a member of the family than as one of the patients.

The other mental health patients were also not badly off, and many of them had their own servants. One of them was a Miss Jones who, when the war began used to open the window and rant out at Hitler. She was always very nice to me, though, and would call me Bri and read to me from the Doctor Doolittle and Barbar the Elephant books. These sessions instilled in me a great love of reading; as an adult, until my eyesight failed, I used to read at least two books a week. I was particularly fond of historical fiction.

One of the most important inhabitants of the household had previously been Edwin Arthur Joseph Augustus Vincent, with whom Granny Deacon formed a very close relationship, which was essentially that between a doctor and a patient. Granny and Mr Vincent had met when she was working at the ICI munitions factory in Widnes,

Mr Vincent

where he was the manager, and had hit it off so well that he moved in to the ménage and lived *in situ* as a paying guest. Unlike many of the other inhabitants, there was nothing wrong with Mr Vincent mentally but he did have some medical ailments, which gave him a slightly misshapen appearance, stooped and needing to wear very strong spectacles. Over time this grew worse. His medical condition was known as acromegaly – something the Elephant Man also suffered from – and Granny was the first person to explain to him the nature of what was wrong, and she also had the courage to tell him how the disease would progress and what awaited him in the future. His head grew very large, he had a hunchback and his hands became like spades, and to compound his suffering the local children would laugh at him, which upset him greatly because he had a very sensitive disposition. He worshipped Granny and the two of them became very close.

Mr Vincent played an important role in my family's life, too. For years, Granny had been renting a place called Rannerdale

Rannerdale Cottage

BRIAN MCELNEY

Ellen Palmer Deacon, Ethel Morris, Mrs Campbell Brown, Mrs Dutton, at 22 The Esplanade, Waterloo (Granny's house)

Cottage near Buttermere in the Lake District and in the mid-1930s, with Granny's encouragement, Mr Vincent first took over the lease and then bought the freehold from its previous owner, a farmer. By the time we arrived back in England, he was living there full-time with his housekeeper Miss Edmondson and had completed some work on the building, including a one-storey extension that turned it into a four bedroom house, although one of the bedrooms was little more than a box room.

Mr Vincent was also a talented gardener and he had meticulously planned and planted a garden that was now in the process of maturing. They agreed that Granny and the rest of us would come to stay whenever we wanted, although there wasn't quite enough room for all of us and we boys would sleep in the gazebo. The house was a T-shaped edifice, with two storeys at the front and one at the rear. We would spend time there during the summer holidays, an idyll for us after the six-hour drive from Liverpool (there were no motorways back then), and when Mr

Vincent died in 1943, he left it to Granny. The ownership of it remains in the family to this day.

This was still a time when the middle class could live in some style. Back in Liverpool, there was a cook, a housemaid and Mrs Dutton, the housekeeper. Other residents included my great aunt Miss Ellen Palmer Deacon, who was Tom's sister. My grandfather was referred to as The Major by the inhabitants of the house who were not actually family but he was so overshadowed by Granny that his personality never shone as hers did. He died two years after our return from Hong Kong.

The Malayan honey bear and the wallaby that we had brought back with us from Hong Kong had gone to Chester Zoo, but we still had Judy the Macaque, a horrible monkey who from time to time tried to take great bites out of me and was cordially loathed by everyone except Granny, who adored her and who was the only person Judy would treat well. She would come out on walks with us, run up a tree and then drop down on Granny's head (she avoided the rest of us) and on one rather horrible occasion, found a frog and tore it apart with her bare hands. On another occasion, Granny took her to the hairdresser in Cockermouth, where she caused pandemonium because she wouldn't allow anyone to touch Granny's hair!

The Sulphur Crested cockatoo (which we had taken to the beach) and a whole host of smaller birds, such as budgerigars, lived in a large aviary in the glass conservatory of the house and you could hear them cheeping away throughout the day. There were various cats and dogs over the years and a parrot called Polly, who became fond of brandy. She had been found unconscious in her cage, and Granny had revived her with a drop from the brandy bottle. Having worked out that this was the route to her snifter she would lie down on the floor and pretend to be ill.

"Oh Ellen," Granny would say, "give the wretched thing some

Rev Robert McElney, Aunt Mary, Aunt Flops, Anne Granny Davison, Harper (behind), Jack

brandy if that's what it wants". And so Polly would get her nip.

We started to settle in. Desmond and I were taught to swim at the public baths near Waterloo. I quite enjoyed it, particularly backstroke, but I was never a strong swimmer and my enthusiasm for diving was very short-lived after a painful belly flop from the topmost diving platform. Desmond, however, persevered. In 1939, Desmond and I were also reunited with our father when he arrived in February to do some further studying. It had been five years since his previous visit to the UK, when he had returned to Hong Kong with two motherless little boys in tow, and now he came back to sit some further gynaecological and midwifery exams at Edinburgh University, as that work had now become the staple of his practice.

In July or August that year, my father took us to Ireland to visit the other side of the family and we spent a week or so with my paternal grandparents in Downpatrick, a journey that was marred by a crossing on the Irish Sea that was so rough and violent I can

COLLECTING CHINA

Jack, Miss McKay, me, Granny Davison, Rev Robert McElney, Mary, Anne and Desmond (on the ground) at The Hill, Downpatrick

remember it to this day. Aunty Mary and Anne joined us on that visit. My father's brother William Harper Campbell Davison McElney, who was to die in World War II, was over from South Africa at the time and this was the only occasion on which I met him. That mouthful of a name came from his two grandfathers, William McElney of Magherabeg near Randalstown, County Antrim, who lived from 1820 to 1885, and Harper Campbell Davison of Primrose Mount, Ballytresna, Randalstown.

Granny Davison, incidentally, came from a wealthy background. She inherited a substantial sum from an uncle, John Davison, who died in the United States, after various family members had emigrated to Augusta (Georgia) in the 1790s. He had become a member of the Georgia legislature, and made his fortune as a cotton factor, and was one of the founders of the First Railroad and Banking Company of Georgia. After the Civil War, the victorious North attempted to confiscate his cotton, only to be told that they could not do so because he had (wisely) retained his

British citizenship. According to another relative, Lady Rosenthal, who had a "grace and favour" apartment at Hampton Court in the 1950s, John Davison Rockefeller was named after him. On his death in 1877, he left US$1 million, a fortune in those days, of which my grandmother received one-twentieth (approximately £10,000) which paid for the education of all her children.

That was really my only contact with my father's parents. And all I can remember is that my great aunt Arabella Hamilton Davison was deaf and shouted a lot and we in turn had to shout into her ear trumpet. Granny Davison would play the piano, accompanied by her cocker spaniel. We were there as the general feeling was that my grandfather wouldn't last much longer and sadly that was right. He died shortly afterwards.

The timing of my father's visit was interesting. War had been on the cards for some time now and shortly after my father returned to these shores, on September 1st, 1939, Germany invaded Poland. Two days later, we were at war. What happened over the next six years affected everyone, each in their different way. In my father's case, a return to Hong Kong was impossible. He wrote to his partners back in the Far East and asked "What shall I do?"

"We'll see you after the war," was the reply.

What my father actually did was to join the RAF, where he served as a medical officer, eventually ending up as a Squadron Leader. Initially he was posted nearby, or at least in the UK, serving in Eastbourne and Scotland, in RAF Coastal Command. But as the war progressed, he was sent much further away to Sekondi-Takoradi in the Western Region of Ghana. Although by then he had come to specialise in gynaecology, he had originally trained as a specialist in tropical medicine and this was going to be very useful in his new role. The Gold Coast, where my grandmother had also worked as a doctor, had become an important staging post in getting planes from America through to the Egyptian

COLLECTING CHINA

desert campaigns. The planes did not at that stage have the range needed to fly very long distances and the narrowest crossing of the Atlantic was between the tip of Brazil and the Gold Coast, which meant they were also able to avoid the Germans in North Africa. My father spent some time there, treating diseases of a type not seen in Europe and serving as a locum in Kano where the local doctor had a pet hunting cheetah, with which my father got on well. My father also served as a locum in another refuelling stop at Até, (in Nigeria), where the aircraft fuel came in by camel. Eventually he was posted back to the UK, where he was based in Bircham Newton in East Anglia.

Back in Liverpool, we didn't see a great deal of him during the war, save when he was home on leave, but we had troubles of our own to contend with. The first eight months of the war are often referred to as the "phoney war", with no major military land operations taking place. But by mid-1940, there was nothing phoney about what the country was going through. Granny's house was only five-hundred yards away from the docks at Bootle, which were a prime target for Hitler's aircraft. That meant that we were a prime target too, and so we used the cellar of the house as a kind of air raid shelter. Great pit props from a nearby mine were installed to make sure the roof didn't cave in, and a couple of enormous, cavernous rooms were converted into sleeping areas. The whole household slept down there and quite apart from the constant threat of bombings, we children were also somewhat unnerved by the décor, which looked like something set up for Hallowe'en, with melons and streamers. Our already very active imaginations went into overdrive.

Our nanny, Miss McKay, who was the daughter of the station master at the village of Rosemarkie in the Black Isle, took us to visit her own parents, as well as on excursions to Tenby. Shortly afterwards she decided that she would marry Willy, the chauffeur.

Desmond and me at Holmwood

This should have been the start of a happy new life for her but, alas, it was the opposite: the war was now raging and the boat in which she and Willy had set sail for Canada was sunk.

This was a tragedy, although we were still really too young to understand. It did, however, necessitate another change in our circumstances. My father paid Granny £500 a year to look after our living expenses and now began to fork out for school fees as well, as the time had come to make the next change to our domestic lives. With no one to look after us properly at home, Desmond and I were enrolled in a prep school called Holmwood, then run by a man called Mr Royds, which was located halfway between Formby and Freshfield. Desmond and I initially attended as day boys, travelling by train from Waterloo on the Southport line. We were unusually young to start, about six and seven, but it was deemed to be the best solution to the problem of two motherless and now nanny-less boys. There was also the feeling that a houseful of much older mental patients was not perhaps the right atmosphere in which to bring up two young chaps. It was the best school in the area, and our fellow pupils included John Moores junior, the son of the founder of the Littlewoods empire, who was four years older than me.

The school was about a mile inland from the sea and boasted huge playing fields. There were extensive grounds, with trees extending back to the dunes, and ponds, where I once saw mating toads. We soon afterwards became weekly boarders, going home just at the weekends, not least because the school was not a target for Hitler's bombs and so we were safer there than we would have been at home. We were housed in dorms, where we messed around as little boys do, engaging in pillow fights and horsing around. But it could be freezing cold.

It was a Spartan place, with no heating to speak of and chill blains in the winter, and because of the war, many of the masters were in fact women or much older men as the younger men were away fighting. Some had a rough time of it. There was one woman who was targeted by some of the boys because she could not maintain discipline. They would do horrible things like positioning buckets of water on the tops of doors when she came into a room. It was a cruel way to behave and I wasn't involved, but the poor woman was pretty hopeless and had no idea how to impose discipline. Most of the other teachers were far more sensible and level-headed in their handling of the boys but Desmond also remembers a lax atmosphere, missing in discipline, with small boys playing tricks on the women. On one occasion white mice popped up out of nowhere, much to our amusement. In those days, of course, slapping with rulers was still permitted.

Even so, I had a traditional classic education in what was then one of the best educational systems in the world. I started to learn French at the age of six, Latin at eight and, slightly more unusually, Greek at eleven. Like so many English prep schools,

BRIAN MCELNEY

Playing cricket at Holmwood

COLLECTING CHINA

Holmwood was keen to educate its pupils in all manner of sports, and although I wasn't much of a cricketer, I did have my moments. On one occasion I caught someone out (in truth, entirely coincidentally – I happened to put my hand up at the exact moment the ball flew into it) and the headmaster, who was umpiring, was so surprised that he pulled the whistle out of his mouth and his false teeth came with it, causing much hilarity among the boys. We played football in the winter and I enjoyed boxing, but never saw myself as a natural sportsman. We continued swimming and also joined the scouts, learning knotting, camping skills and map-reading, all adding to the strong sense of self-reliance that was to be reinforced as we grew up and eventually began travelling on our own. We also rode ponies until we were about fourteen, although I developed a cautious attitude towards horses after that.

I did, however, have rather a good voice. I joined the choir and over time became its leader. I was such an eager participant that I probably sang too much and ended up by over-straining my voice. The choir was also the occasion of one of those moments that is absolutely mortifying to the young. I was in the middle of an impassioned rendition of "Hark, Hark! The lark at Heaven's gate sings" when my voice suddenly and unexpectedly broke, with at least 150 people watching. It is the kind of experience that many a young boy will have to undergo but traumatic when it happens to you, nonetheless. And it can't have done my reputation at the school much harm: I ended up as head boy.

Occasionally we saw my father. Once, he drove us from Liverpool to Rannerdale and kept us occupied on that long drive by singing snatches from the Mikado – when I hear "A Wandering Minstrel I" or "Tit Willow", it always makes me think of him. Having received a gold medal at Campbell College, Belfast for maths, he also set us mathematical problems such as the following: two trains a mile long are passing each other, each travelling at

60mph. How long would the track take to clear? The answer is one minute and after this extra-curricular tuition it is notable that I got a distinction for elementary maths in my School Certificate.

Weekends and holidays were spent in Liverpool or Rannerdale but the Esplanade continued to be rocked by bombs aimed at the docks and anti-aircraft batteries nearby. On one occasion a bomb exploded four doors away and shattered the entire glass conservatory, including the aviary, killing all the birds. It was not an ideal place to live by this time and shortly afterwards matters were taken out of our hands.

In 1943 there was more upheaval on the home front. Mr Vincent died and left Rannerdale to Granny, while at the same time the house in Liverpool was requisitioned to be used by the American forces. The household decided to move to Rannerdale full-time and so began the process of downsizing from a huge house to a more normally-sized one, with much of the furniture being sold and more disruption for us all. Only one member of the household staff, Mrs Dutton, came with us, along with my bedridden great aunt, Ellen Palmer Deacon.

Although it was wartime and rationing was in place, in actual fact it didn't really affect us out there in the Lake District because we were living in lush and plentiful countryside that provided a veritable feast for two small boys and the associated household. There was a farm next door from whom we got milk, butter and eggs. Mrs Dutton would bake bread and scones and I would watch the slow rise of the dough after it had been kneaded in the baking tins on the hearth before it went into the oven. When it came out we would eat it, still warm, covered in butter and jam, so delicious that the family would often polish off a whole loaf in the course of an afternoon.

Out in the garden, we grew strawberries, raspberries, gooseberries, apples, Victoria plums and red and black currants

COLLECTING CHINA

Jack and Rev Robert McElney
Me, Granny Davison, Desmond, Mary and Anne

and beyond the boundaries of the garden hedgerows and the local woods would yield up plentiful crops of blackberries and blueberries. What we didn't eat straightaway Mrs Dutton would make into jams and marmalades and store them in the coolness of the larder, in those pre-refrigerator days. Not that the coolness preserved everything: once we found small white worms amid the raspberries and complained to Granny. "Not to worry, they're just another form of raspberry," she replied.

We also had bantams in the garden, which would provide us with eggs. Granny Deacon was not soft-hearted with people, but she certainly was with animals and intervened on one occasion when Mrs Dutton found a cockroach and was about to put it on the fire. Granny carefully put it out of the window, out, she thought, of harm's way, until there was a cacophony of clucking and flapping of wings as the bantams all raced to lay claim to what they clearly thought was a treat. The cock bantam won and Granny was horrified.

It was a blissful place to be a child. Rannerdale was not a target for the bombing and so gone were the days of cowering in the cellar, and when we returned to the cottage during the summer holidays, it was a wonderful place. We ran wild among the lakes, climbing mountains and rolling rocks down them to see how far they would go, behaviour that would be termed anti-social these days. But the Lake District in those days was a wilderness, practically inaccessible to the casual visitor and so there was no one to see us as we climbed the trees to rob birds' nests and tickled trout in the stream that bordered our garden. We fished in the lakes and cycled everywhere.

Of course the Lakes are famous for rain and storms and Rannerdale lay in a valley where the caldera of the hills creates a phenomenon known as "helm wind," howling and bouncing back and forth to such a degree that it builds into a frightening crescendo. It can be so terrifying that the Saxons and their Viking allies holed up at Buttermere used it to defeat William Rufus's knights when they tried to pass through the valley – the knights thought they were being pursued by banshees. On days like this, we would stay in and I would pour over my stamp collection, or play cards or a game called L'attack. I was already an avid reader and would spend many hours hunched over my books. They were idyllic times for a small child.

But soon there was to be yet more change. The end of the war was upon us, my father returned to Hong Kong where he was demobbed and Desmond and I prepared for our next school, where one of the masters was to have such an influence on me that he would ultimately set me on track for the greatest passion of my life – collecting art.

CHAPTER 4
Picnics And Pictures

Eventually the war came to an end, but so, too, did that part of our childhood that had centred around Granny and her household, not least as various family members and assorted friends and guests had begun to pass away. The Major had died in a nursing home in Waterloo in 1940 and in August 1942 Mr Vincent followed him as a result of a haemorrhage from his pituitary gland. Miss Deacon, my grandfather's spinster sister, who had moved with us to Rannerdale also went to the next life in 1946 at the age of 94. On April 18th 1947, Granny died at the age of 76 after a nasty accident involving being scalded by a burst hot water bottle. Her nephew Mackenzie Stewart, by now working in Carlisle Hospital, did all he could to save her, but her burns were too serious to recover from. We children were taken to say goodbye. She left Rannerdale and all its contents to my father and what little was left over went in trust for my brother and me.

But the loss of beloved relatives aside, this was not a melancholy time for Desmond and I: quite the contrary. We started spending part of the summer holidays in Great Bedwyn with Aunty Mary and Anne in 1944 and again in 1946, the year I started at Marlborough, a traditional English public school founded in 1843 which was chosen for its proximity to Great Bedwyn. Aunty

COLLECTING CHINA

Mary was by now our legal guardian and I suspect she was a little concerned that we had been allowed to run wild in the Lake District and needed to have the rough edges smoothed out before we were allowed back into polite society. She paid attention to our table manners (or at least, forced us to) and corrected our use of language. This was a time when Received Pronunciation was important and could actually have affected the way we got on in life. But our time there was also magical, again redolent of a lost world.

Aunty Mary and Anne lived in Little Chase, a modern house that had been completed just before the war, perched half way up a hill with views stretching out over the rolling fields of Wiltshire and, in the distance, the River Dun. Aunty Mary was a keen gardener, as Anne was to become after her, and at that point was still engaged in constructing the garden, allowing an open lawn to lead on to the views across the fields and a row of trees, mainly silver birch, to shield the house from the road. It took a while before the garden was complete.

There were shrubs planted at the front, and the green fingers clearly ran in the family as Anne was later to create a beautiful garden of her own, as well as contributing a great deal to developing the gardens at Rannerdale. The village was close to both Marlborough and Hungerford in what is now classed as an Area of Outstanding Natural Beauty and Conservation, in other words somewhere that was perfect to bring up children.

After my McElney grandparents died, in 1943 the enterprising Aunty Mary visited Downpatrick and appropriated two antique bicycles, which were named after their previous owners: Isabella (another great aunt, Isabella McElney, who died in 1936) and Arabella Hamilton Davison (who had gone into a home before my grandparents' death). Aunty Mary got them to London and found a taxi, the driver of which thought she was taking them to the

B1 House rugger team, Marlborough

Science Museum, but instead she took them to Paddington Station and from there to her own home. Aunt Mary commandeered Arabella, which we believed was originally made in the 1890s, and used her to cycle to work – like everyone of working age she was engaged in war work – which was a common way of getting about at that time as rationing was still in place and petrol was hard to come by. Unfortunately, like many an old-age pensioner Arabella was feeling her age and one day snapped completely in half. Aunty Mary did actually have a car as well, a 1937/8 Austin 7 which she bought at the motor show in Olympia in London for £36. It kept her going well into the 1950s, when it was sold for £50, despite having caught fire shortly before the sale!

During our visit there in 1944 during the holidays, I rode Isabella, which was thought to date from about 1896, and learned to cope with the eccentricities of a bicycle that would have done a flesh-and-blood dowager of the same name proud. For a start the brakes caused horrible complications. The front brake was quite a way down the handlebar shaft, which meant that it was almost impossible for me to reach, while the rear brake worked by pedalling backwards and it took me a little while to master the talent. The first time I skidded downhill on Isabella, I couldn't use the rear brake, with the result that I went straight over a bank and into the trunk of a large oak tree, which knocked me out cold. But I persevered and eventually mastered the art of riding her without coming a cropper.

Although the war was going on, it was actually a very happy time, looking back, with we children afforded a kind of freedom that many youngsters are denied today. Days were spent walking, bicycling and picnicking in the lovely countryside nearby. We would pick blackberries in the hedgerows of Savernake Forest and go fishing and collect watercress in the Kennett and Avon canal, or swim in the canal where water reeds and fish would brush past our legs.

The house had a one-acre garden and there was plenty to see there: grass snakes and slow worms, butterflies and humming bird hawk moths visiting the catmint, where they would hover and drink the nectar, just as an actual humming bird would. We climbed trees, staged snail and slug races and learned the names of the butterflies and larger moths. Racing around in the fresh air all day meant that we were far healthier than today's children: although I caught many an infection as a child, as an adult I never had any problems except for the odd chest infection until, for other reasons, my health broke down when I was 50.

Anne would sometimes accompany us but she was a few years older than us and in any case would get very cross with us when we behaved like the teenage boys we now were. When we discovered she hated daddy long legs and spiders we collected a group of them and deposited them in her bedroom, which did not go down well.

BRIAN MCELNEY

Rationing was still in existence and we didn't eat a great deal, but what we did tasted every bit as delicious as the many gourmet meals I came to eat in later life in Hong Kong. Aunt Mary was an excellent cook and managed to make even the simplest fare an indulgence. One typical dish was a baked potato cut open and served with a soft boiled egg inside it, a great treat known as a "spud Murphy". It can't really have been the case that the sun shone every day but it does so in my memory, a golden idyll before the responsibilities of adulthood began to take their toll.

Our love of cycling was put to the test a few years later. One Easter holiday we cycled from Marlborough, where I was by now at school and of which more anon, to stay with John Robert Holdrich Fisher, always known as Robin, who was my best friend at Marlborough, and his family at Ottery St Mary in Devon. Robin, who died on June 12th 1998, was the fifth generation of surgeons, continued from father to son from Napoleonic times. He became the senior consultant orthopaedic surgeon at Walsall General Hospital, and some years after we left school his eldest child Robert, who also became a doctor, became the second of my many godchildren. Robin was clearly very much loved by the people of Walsall, judging by the orations at his funeral. But I am getting ahead of myself.

We cycled on to Torquay where we stayed with Tom Deacon's cousin Ethel Morris, a great favourite with Granny Deacon. Ethel had just got married to a man called Kerslake, who managed the Cockington estate, a village and country house called Cockington Court, which had at one point been very popular with Agatha Christie, to the extent that she dedicated her book "Why Didn't They Ask Evans?" to Christopher Mallock who once owned the house. We stayed with them for a week and in the course of so doing went to see another of Tom's cousins, Annie Ambrose Andrews, at Mannamead in Plymouth. Annie was by this time a widow, her late husband having at one point been Lord Mayor of Plymouth. We then cycled back to the Lake District, staying in youth hostels along the way, which took about five or six days.

We were already unusually well-travelled for children of our generation and became more so after the end of the war. Apart from our trip to Northern Ireland, we had stayed in England for the duration but travel was getting easier again and so in 1946 we went to Saas-Fee in Switzerland to learn to ski, a sport Desmond became very accomplished in although I was never that keen. The trip was organised by a young Canadian master at Marlborough and a number of our fellow students came along: this was our introduction to ice hockey, as well. Saas-Fee is near the Italian border and is famous for its geographical proximity to the "four-thousanders", in other words mountains that rise more than 4,000 meters above sea level.

One of our fellow travellers was Mary Stewart, the youngest daughter of Thomas Bruce Stewart, Granny's youngest brother – Granny was the eldest of ten and he was fourteen years her junior. We had met Great Uncle Bruce in Colombo and Mary, who was my late mother's cousin, was studying at Cheltenham Ladies' College at the time but asked to come along; about a decade later, her son Clive Bennett became my first godchild.

The resort was nothing like the sophisticated locations you see today: this was only a year after the war and facilities were primitive, and there was only one ski lift. Foreign travel was very different from what it is today. We were only allowed to take £50 in spending money but although there were exchange controls in place, my father never had any problem funding foreign holidays because although Hong Kong was technically subject to exchange controls as part of the sterling area, in practice consent was usually given with no restriction. Great Uncle Bruce, who had just retired, also had no difficulties in getting funds.

BRIAN MCELNEY

In 1946, I had left Holmwood to go on to Marlborough, followed a year later by Desmond. I was by now fourteen and had been boarding since the age of eight, so it wasn't that big a change to me, but Marlborough was a civilised place, in the middle of beautiful countryside, and I saw a good deal of it when I went cross-country running, which we would do for miles in all directions. We had bicycles too, although slightly newer than the one I had been accustomed to!

Marlborough College is at the western end of the wide main street of Marlborough, and the original Georgian structure was the principal coaching inn for those travelling to Bath in the eighteenth century. English public schools are made up of houses: Desmond and I were initially in A house, which was exactly that, a house where we lived during our school year and where we were looked after by Dames, who attended to the housekeeping side of things and made sure we were keeping well. All boys were there for the first three terms but despite the lovely surrounding scenery the view from A house was rather bleak.

I then moved to B1 house, a Victorian edifice which housed boys from the age of 13 to 18 and is found at the centre of the campus opposite New Court, again with not much of a view. Designed by the Victorian architect Edward Blore, it was one of the first custom-built boarding houses for any school in the country and has produced some very eminent old boys, including the poet John Betjeman and the travel writer Bruce Chatwin, although neither was a contemporary of mine. Desmond, meanwhile, moved to C1 house, which was in the original Georgian section looking out over a wide green space which was surrounded by a high yew hedge. Much to our delight, it was rumoured once to have been a duelling ground.

I started off in the form known as Upper IV but progressed quite quickly. After the first term I got top marks and was

COLLECTING CHINA

promoted, as it were, to Shell (Year 9) and after another term went up to Hundred, where it was compulsory to stay for three terms and where I took what was then known as the School Certificate awarded by the Oxford and Cambridge joint board, at the time the most testing of the various exam boards. I got a distinction in elementary maths and credits in a range of subjects including advanced mathematics, history, geography, Latin, Greek, English Language and Literature, and French. In the summer I played tennis or went cycling in nearby Savernake Forest and Bedwyn. Discipline was of the old school: I once got six of the best for missing a cross-country run and when the house master caught me saying that it hadn't hurt, he gave me another six with a cane. This type of punishment has been completely eradicated from British schools these days but it didn't do me or any of my fellow students any harm – boys need discipline and have to be taught to obey the rules.

My father remained a largely absent figure, but Desmond and I did spend six weeks with him in 1949 when we visited him in Hong Kong. This was the first time I was to fly in an aeroplane and the conditions were almost unbelievably luxurious compared to how people travel today. The journey took five days and I loved every minute of it. We flew on an Empire Flying Boat, a four-engined monoplane designed to travel between the colonies as well as Bermuda and New York, which took off and landed on the water: we sat in comfortable chairs and benches facing each other across tables and passed the time playing cards. The flying boat travelled at about 200 miles an hour and so it was a much slower journey than it is today: it was full of other children flying back to Hong Kong to visit their families and we chatted to them, all of us full of excitement not only with the prospect of seeing our families but at travelling in a machine which took us up into the clouds.

The plane set off from Portsmouth and our first port of call was

Catania, Sicily, where we spent the night in a hotel. From there it was on to another overnight stop in Alexandria, followed by a refuelling stop in Bahrain, which was extremely hot and humid as it had just received its annual rainfall, and on to Karachi, part of the newly-established Pakistan, where we spent a night in Nissan huts, surrounded by the desert. Then we were on to Calcutta, where we stayed in the Great Eastern Hotel, Rangoon and Bangkok, where we stayed in the old Oriental Hotel, now the Mandarin Oriental and one of the best in the world. I was to stay there on several occasions over the years. There was only one frightening moment during the voyage and that was when we took off from the Chao Phraya river in Bangkok: a small boat appeared out of nowhere and shot across our path, forcing the pilot to pull sharply back on the joystick, essentially leapfrogging the boat as we rose briefly into the air, coming down on the other side of the sampan and continuing to accelerate up the river as we reached real take-off speed. It must have been a common enough occurrence but left us feeling shaky and we were glad when we landed in Hong Kong later that day.

Hong Kong was much as I had remembered it, although I'd been so young when we left that my memories were vague: it still had the small town colonial feel to it; the economic miracle of the future was yet to take off. Over the next few weeks we kept bumping into people we had met on the flight, all relishing their short time with their parents before they were to be sent back to the UK. We amused ourselves by playing golf at Shek O, then and now one of Hong Kong's most exclusive country clubs, and we also played at Deep Water Bay and Fanling. Perhaps I was put off my stroke at that last as we spotted snakes nearby and I did not take to the sport, never playing again in Hong Kong after that. We also went swimming from the Shell launch: Dick Frost, the head of Shell, was a friend of my father's and one of Desmond's godparents.

That visit was also to provide a souvenir. My father had recently delivered male twins to the wife of Aw Ho, who was part of the family that developed Tiger Balm ointment and thus worth a fortune. Thanks to my father (and his own wife), Aw Ho now had male heirs. When he heard that my father's two sons were also in Hong Kong, he wanted to give us a present and asked for a suggestion. My father mentioned that we might appreciate suitcases for when we travelled back on the flying boat. Aw Ho did indeed give us something that was meant for travel, but travel in the traditional Chinese style, and we were duly presented with two camphor wood chests.

That trip was the first of several excursions in the school holidays. We continued to spend time at Great Bedwyn, but my father felt we shouldn't spend all our time with relatives and so there was youth hostelling around the UK and further excursions across Europe where we stayed in pensions. There were some notable incidents: on one occasion when Desmond was 17 and I a year older, we were driving across Paris, Desmond at the wheel, trying to find a place to stay.

I was reading the map and despite many years studying French took us first to the Hotel de Ville and then the Hotel des Invalides. But all was not lost: when we did finally find a place to stay we made our way to the Folies Bergères. We toured the Loire and visited chateaux and travelled the railways, recording our experiences with an old box camera. In Brittany we sampled the wonderful shellfish. No one worried about the fact that communication was difficult, and all this unescorted travel when we were still in our teens made us extremely independent.

And we certainly had some adventures. Another trip to Spain resulted in a warning from the Guarda Civil in San Sebastian that our swimming trunks were too scanty. We travelled across Spain via Zaragosa to Gerona to see the Black Madonna and from there to Sant Feliu de Guixols on the Costa Brava, where I encountered a bedbug, the only time in a lifetime of travel that I have ever done so. Our return to the UK was via Cerbère and Carcassonne.

We also did a lot of travelling with Aunty Mary and Anne. In the summer of 1950, the year I left school, Desmond and I visited Scandinavia, taking in Denmark, Sweden and Norway and travelling to Esberg with our bicycles. We cycled from there to Copenhagen, where Anne was working for the British Council and Aunty Mary was already *in situ*: the four of us journeying on to Malmo in Sweden and from there to Lake Vasa with the bicycles in tow. Anne and Mary took a boat on the Gota Canal to Stockholm and we followed a day or two later, after cycling to Jonkoping, where we witnessed a glorious display of the Northern Lights. We arrived in Stockholm where we had arranged to meet them – I remember an excellent lunch in the town hall at the Golden Fleece restaurant – and then Desmond and I continued on our own to Hamar and Lillehammer while Anne had to return to her job in Copenhagen, having only one week's leave, accompanied by Aunty Mary.

Next on the agenda was a drive up Galdøpiggen, the highest mountain in Norway, a nerve-wracking route with its hairpin bends, but the driver was obviously an experienced one and so we felt in safe hands. From there we progressed on to Leikanger on the Sogne Fjord, where we took a boat to Bergen. We then took the train from Bergen to Oslo, making a temporary stop at Myrdal to take a detour to Flam, which we reached by rail, a beautiful area I have since visited twice again. Finally it was on to Oslo itself, where my lifelong habit of visiting museums in whichever city I should happen to be in resulted in the sighting of a Viking longboat. Finally we returned to the UK, to Newcastle, on board a ship.

COLLECTING CHINA

We holidayed with my father on occasion too, visiting Celerina over the Christmas and New Year of 1950-51, the home of the Cresta bob sleigh run next door to St Moritz. My father brought Fiona Anderson with him, the daughter of Dr Anderson, one of the partners in the firm, and the family reunion was a very happy one, with Anne there too along with Anthony Evans, the son of Don Brittan Evans, senior partner of Johnson Stokes & Master at that time. There was much hilarity when my father, who had not skied before, went straight into a snowdrift with a cigarette still in his mouth.

But all these were entertainments during the holidays and the real business of study was still going on. Back at school I moved to the Classical Vth to study Latin and Greek, subjects I chose because they presented a greater challenge than anything else, as well as Latin and Greek history, prose and verse. We also all had to opt for a half subject outside our speciality and in my case, I chose three maths-related subjects: statics, dynamics and astronomy. But it was while I was studying the classics that I met the teacher who was to have a real impact on the course of my life. They say that one outstanding teacher can make a huge difference to an individual student and that was certainly the case with me: the master in question was named Louis Ferrand Audemars – referred to by the boys as Pont Audemar after the famous Normandy bridge – and he was an enormously cultivated man, with a vast range of knowledge that extended far beyond his chosen field. He was Classics and Art History master at Marlborough from 1924 to 1952.

He did not just teach the classics, he taught an understanding of the fine arts as well. Every week, we had two periods devoted to art appreciation and it was those two periods that had a far greater impact on my life than anything else taught at school. Every week he would pin postcards or pictures of Western art to the blackboard, some of the greatest pictures in the canon, and would explain to us the importance of the artist or school of artists being covered. He would then tell us to pick one painting we particularly liked and write an essay about why we liked it, something that you might say became a lifelong habit as many decades later, when I had started to build up my collection properly in Hong Kong, I continued to write about art and still do, contributing to, among other things, the journal of the institution I founded, the Museum of East Asian Art.

This was my first exposure to some of the greatest art in the world, much of which I was to see later in the course of my travels, although everything that we looked at was entirely European, as only European art was taught at the time. However, it was a superb grounding and the fact that I have a photographic memory, which was to come in extremely useful when I started building my own collection, meant that I remembered my first sightings of these works perfectly when I went on to see the real thing. Audemars showed us *The Doge* by Titian, *Lady With An Ermine* by Leonardo da Vinci, which I saw in Krakow in 2007, *Primavera* by Botticelli, Duccio's *Maesta*, which I also saw later in Sienna and of course Leonardo's *Last Supper*. I also still have a vivid memory of being shown two Velasquez paintings, *Don Carlos* and *Las Meninas*, a painting of the Spanish royal family children (who were unfortunately no oil paintings themselves), and I was also very much struck by El Greco. Audemars taught us to look at colour, light and shade, perspective, and where the artist placed figures – in other words, composition. We started with Byzantine pictures of the saints, which employed no perspective, moved on to Giotto, one of the first to start using perspective and finally ended up with the Impressionists. We also looked at Greek pottery and sculpture, and another master gave lectures to the whole school on other artistic subjects such as architecture, garden design and landscaping, learning about such figures as Capability Brown.

Audemars was a superb teacher and like all truly inspirational educators took a personal interest in his students, inviting us to his home and showing us his own beautifully-appointed drawing room, full of lovely antiques. We were very impressed. "Of course you cannot furnish a room, a drawing room, properly for under £10,000," he told us when we complimented him on his taste. Given that this was around 1950, we were shocked to the core, although when I later came to furnish a drawing room myself some decades later, I found the figure to be closer to £70,000…

It is entirely possible that my contemporaries at Marlborough would have proven to be a very accomplished set of people even without a master like Audemars, but it certainly turned out to be a very distinguished class and the effect he had on his students was reflected in the obituary published in *The Marlburian* after his death in 1954. "Some of them [his students] declared that their whole outlook on life materially altered as a result of the hours spent in studying art and sculpture and their relationship to civilised life, subjects which were his particular interest," it read.

That was so in my case and conceivably others of my peers, two in particular who were younger than me (I was then seventeen) but had been put up a few years. Among my contemporaries was Peter Brooke, then fourteen, later Baron Brooke of Sutton Mandeville, who became Secretary of State for Culture, Sport and the Arts, and went on to be the first master of the Art Dealers, Collectors and Curators City of London Guild, founded in 2006. I joined immediately after its foundation and am a Freeman of the Guild to this day. Another was Sir Nicholas Goodison, another champion of the arts as Chairman of the Art Fund and of the Courtauld Institute, and author of several books on decorative arts. It might be coincidence, but surely a strong one, that two men so heavily involved in the arts should have been educated by the same man – as, of course, was I.

In the meantime, during my last year at Marlborough I shared a study with the head boy of B1, Julian Hurd, the brother of Douglas Hurd who later became Foreign Secretary, along with one other boy. Julian was a very impressive speaker but was very tragically killed in an accident a few years after leaving school. I went on to a class taught by Mr Shaw and eventually achieved my Higher Certificate, with good grades in Latin and Greek history, still one of my favourite subjects, although the rest of it didn't come up to scratch, for the simple reason that I have never performed well in exams, especially when a subject didn't interest me. But all too soon that period came to an end and it was time to decide how I, too, would make my own way out in the world.

CHAPTER 5
BEDSIT LAND

AFTER LEAVING MARLBOROUGH there was some talk about my going to university, but on the whole it was thought best that I straight away pursue a qualification and it was decided that it would be in the law. Despite coming from generations of doctors on both sides of my family, my father was keen that I should not follow suit.

"I can't even go to my own parties," he told me, explaining that over and again it had happened that one of his expat patients had gone into labour on the evenings that he had planned to enjoy himself. I therefore decided to become a solicitor and Desmond an accountant, a good way of splitting up the two professions between us. And so I moved to London, a strange period in my life, where I made my first purchase as a collector and qualified as a solicitor, but never really settled down. It was an interim period between school and my professional life.

There were two ways of becoming a solicitor at the time: three years at university followed by three years doing Articles – six in total – or five years doing Articles and taking the Law Society's exams. I chose the latter option and went to work for Gilbert Rathbone Whitehead, the son of Sir Rowland Edward Whitehead, at a firm called Blyth Dutton Wright & Bennett, based at Gresham House on Old Broad Street, not far from the Bank of

England. It specialised in conveyancing and estates and I was to gain considerable experience in those areas, as well as becoming involved in some litigation, as the firm were agents for Privy Council work from Australia, very unusual for the time and one of the reasons I wanted to work for them. One of the founders of the firm was Sir Frederick Dutton, who was born in Adelaide and co-incidentally educated at Marlborough. His own father had twice been Premier of the first South Australian Parliament and was for several years Agent-General for the State in London. We did a lot of business with Australia, although of course in those days it took two weeks for a letter to get there and two weeks for it to return and so work was done at nothing like the speed it can be now.

The option of returning to Hong Kong at that point was ruled out as, at the time, it was impossible to qualify as a solicitor there. My father paid £500 for me to do Articles, which was quite a considerable sum at the time and as I would not receive payment for the duration, he gave me an allowance of £45 a month, about the same as a clerk would have earned. Like everyone who worked in the City back then, my uniform consisted of pinstriped trousers, dark grey jacket (I always refused to wear black), rolled umbrella and bowler hat. This dress code gradually became less formal as time went on, and even the bowler hat had gone by the time I finished Articles. The firm was very respectable indeed, although looking back now it seems very old-fashioned. The building dated from about 1910 and still had old-style lifts, and doors with half-glass windows in them. There were high ceilings and whirring fans and clerks and piles of paper everywhere; the partners all had their secretaries and the atmosphere was buzzing and highly charged, be it almost unrecognisable to the modern world.

Our hours were 10am to 5pm and initially, a lot of my time was spent getting copies of wills or delivering papers for probate. I also attended law school, two long sessions of four months each, where I learned the theory of the law while Blyth Dutton taught me the practicalities. Back in the firm I spent time in each of the different departments: probate, debt collection, litigation, traffic cases and so on. I shared offices with the clerks and a son of one of the partners, who was also articled. One of our larger clients was Vítkovice Steel, a big steel works in Czechoslovakia for whom much of the work involved estates and elective litigation. It was a good all-round training.

Like so many young people who come to London to make a career for themselves, my life was slightly itinerant. I had a series of short-lived occupancies before settling down, first at 30 Loudon Road in St John's Wood, which was a B&B-type place with its own cook and a Group Captain Gordon-Finlayson who also lived there. After that it was downhill for a bit, however, for it was followed by a short stay at a place near Finchley Road tube station and from there to Ridgemont Gardens, a flat near Tottenham Court Road which is where the famous Heal's department store is based, where I bought a little souvenir that I have to this day. 1953 was the year of the Coronation and I watched the proceedings from the top of a building on Northumberland Avenue, which overlooks Trafalgar Square and thus the procession that went on to Westminster Abbey. I bought from Heal's a glass Coronation Goblet for the princely sum of £9. This was a small fortune at the time, nearly a quarter of my monthly allowance, but it was a beautiful piece of glass, and a limited edition piece with red, white and blue filaments in the stem, and has come to assume some rarity value.

Finally, in 1953, I moved to a garden flat at 44 Lexham Gardens with, indeed, a garden, where my father had bought a three-year lease for £500. Considerably more settled now, I rented out a bedroom to an acquaintance of mine called Gerald Weill, another student whose parents lived in Hong Kong, and with him visited Fowey one summer where his mother had a holiday home. It was a lovely area, preserved in my memory because I caught several mackerel there. Rannerdale Cottage was by now rented out at £90 a year, an income that came to me, supplementing the allowance from my father, and the income derived from the £1,000 or so capital inherited from my mother and grandmother. The flat was crammed full of furniture, which largely originated from Rannerdale, including a few good antiques.

Life was comfortable, although not luxurious. When I first moved to London, rationing was still in place and so our options were somewhat limited. Sometimes I'd eat at a local café for about two shillings and sixpence; I was also rather good at whipping up a curry, which I enjoyed doing. No-one ever taught boys to cook back then and I had certainly never received any formal training, but Aunt Flops, with whom I now spent many weekends, had taken a course in Edinburgh to become a Cordon Bleu cook, so I picked something up from watching her. Whenever she cooked, though, the kitchen turned into a disaster area, unlike Aunty Mary, who was pristine in her habits. I was more in the Aunt Flops mode. Great Uncle Bruce and his wife Marie, who was also a good cook, were living fairly close by in Earl's Court, with their two younger daughters, Yvonne Stewart and Mary Stewart, and I frequently managed to arrive on their doorstep at mealtimes. One form of constant entertainment was the cinema: I used to go to the Classic on Baker Street and saw most of the good films of the day, including all the classic Marx Brothers outings.

I saw my father intermittently and in 1953, when I turned 21, he came to the UK and took me out to a celebratory lunch at The Savoy, where he presented me with a gold watch. The occasion was memorable for another reason, too: there was a performer present who was good at swiping objects out of people's pockets without them realising and then presenting them. He summoned me up on stage and swiped a comb out of my pocket. To my great embarrassment it had only three prongs.

During my Articles I worked on a case which stimulated my interest in genealogy, involving the estate of Edward (I think that was his Christian name) Caporn, deceased. This man had died in about 1850 leaving a will mandating three consecutive life interests but failed to make any disposition of the property after the life interests had run their course, or to make a residuary bequest which would have included such remainder interest. This meant there was an intestacy as to that residue. The deceased's property at his death was copyhold in the manor of Stepney and inheritance on intestacy of such property was according to the custom of the Manor, which we found to be Gavelkind as commonly applied in Kent, under which sons inherited equally.

Although all three sons had survived the testator (their father), by the time Blyth Dutton became involved, the deceased's three sons were long dead, but their one-third interest in the trust fund concerned would have formed part of each son's estate and pass under his will, or intestacy if there was no will, and the laws of intestacy to be applied would be those in force at the son's death. And so on until living heirs were identified. This was a mammoth task and heir hunters took it in hand. The case instilled in me the importance of including a residuary bequest in any will.

This sparked an interest in my own family's background and so I joined the Society of Genealogists and spent many hours in their library, based at Harrington Gardens, near where I lived, digging into my own past. Because I was spending so much time running errands around London (without actually being paid) I also took the opportunity to do some of my own work and so I would often take time out to continue my own research into my family tree.

Shortly after starting Articles I looked into the possibility of doing an external LLB (Bachelor of Laws) at London University

Me and Desmond in London in our 20s

but I discovered my School Certificate had not been registered at London in time and so I would have had to do their entrance exam, which rather put me off. It later emerged that I was far from being alone in this position and some years later London told me that if I took the intermediate exam and passed, they would waive the entrance exam requirement. I agreed to this and I did pass, but by that time I had reached the final stages of my Law Society exams and I knew I was going to accept a job offer in Hong Kong, so I decided to dispense with the LLB.

I had time off at the weekends and when not at the Society of Genealogists or the Newspaper Library at Colindale (another valuable resource), I often went to Shiplake-on-Thames, near Henley, to visit Aunt Flops and her husband, Francis William Davies, who died in 1955. The two lived in slight chaos in a house called Sonningdene with a scatter-brained Red Setter called Micky, to which they had moved after the war from a flat at 26 Cranley Gardens, near Gloucester Road tube station in London and in the same area where I was now living. Both came from the Victorian era; Aunt Flops entering this world in 1893 and Francis in 1885.

Francis came from a very interesting background: he had originally studied to be a doctor but when his own father died unexpectedly, he was forced to drop his studies in order to earn a living. He took a job as the manager of a rubber plantation, first in Sumatra and subsequently in Malaysia, where he ended up with his own plantation of about 2,000 acres. He was a man ahead of his time: the workers were not well-treated back then and he was the first manager to provide midwife and gynaecological facilities for the women working on the coolie lines.

Francis made and lost a couple of fortunes in his lifetime, which gave him an insight into business that he was to pass on to me. He had missed a business opportunity when he was offered a hundred-yard stretch of seafront property in Miami at the depth of the Depression and unfortunately declined it – it would be worth a fortune now. He married my aunt in 1933 at a time when he was doing well. He had invested in mines in South Africa, the west Witwatersrand mine, where he literally and metaphorically hit gold. He then put his money into gold mines in Tanganyika in the mid-1930s but unfortunately his partners made off with the cash.

After the war, he discovered his rubber plantation had been destroyed and so sold out, which was when he bought Sonningdene. Their marriage was an eventful one from the start: they travelled around South Africa where they visited Uncle Harper, and went on to the Falkland Islands and then to South America, where they found themselves thrown into jail in Bolivia – although only for a day – because it turned out that their visa had been signed by someone who had once been declared a traitor in Bolivia.

It was Francis who taught me about investing and stocks and shares, and so I made my first tentative moves into the stock market. He passed on the received wisdom such as "Sell in May and go away and come back on St Leger's Day", Rockefeller's advice always to take a profit if your investment has gone up by ten percent (I didn't always follow this) and the knowledge that you only have to be right 52 percent of the time to do well. Many of the stocks I bought related to companies that are now defunct, for example Home & Colonial Stores, once one of the UK's largest retail chains and now no more. I also invested in Shell Transport and Trading, which is now Royal Dutch Shell, and Banir Rubber. In those days, plantations growing the likes of tea, coffee, rubber and palm oil constituted a big part of the market, whereas now of course their impact is very small.

In 1951 Aunt Flops, Aunty Mary and I had travelled to Randalstown, County Antrim, to attend the funeral of Great Uncle William McElney, my grandfather's younger brother, a farmer

*Uncle Francis William Davies
(Flops' husband)*

and the remnant of another age as he was born in 1866. We stayed at a local pub during the proceedings and Aunt Flops showed me around: William owned two properties, a pleasant little cottage called Magherabeg, where his parents William and Agnes (née Curry) had lived and where he too was living at the time of his death, as well as a large establishment nearby called Sharvogues House, which sat on 150 acres of land amid mature trees. This house had allegedly been built for an illegitimate son of Lord O'Neill, who had been the major landowner in the area and my great uncle, helped by my grandparents, had managed to acquire the two properties under a Land Act that enabled tenant farmers to buy the freehold on generous terms. The sum he paid for the two of them was £950 back in 1895.

William was an eccentric bachelor who never married and who was the subject of many anecdotes. Sharvogues had been requisitioned during the war and had fallen into a terrible state of disrepair by the time of his death, so much so that the floor in the drawing room was six inches lower at one end than the other and the pediment over the front door looked as if it might drop off at any moment.

William's funeral was the type of occasion not often seen these days. When we got there his body was in a glass-topped coffin in Magherabeg's drawing room. A large number of locals had gathered for the occasion to view the body before the cortège set off for the church in nearby Randalstown, followed by the large troupe of locals, one of whom was carrying a scythe. It was an older style of Northern Irish funeral that you don't see nowadays and as for the properties – a local resident bought them and demolished Sharvogues for scrap, while cutting down the trees for timber, but Magherabeg still exists.

Of course I still visited Aunt Mary, and would stay with her when I was revising for my exams as she was very good at keeping my nose to the grindstone, or for longer periods away from work. My other great interest during the London years was art. Even then I was interested in Chinese art because of my Hong Kong background and I was given as a Christmas present a book by W.B. Honey "The Ceramic Art of China and other Countries of the Far East" which totally absorbed my interest. I started visiting some of the great museums of London and making my first tentative steps as a collector, too. There was a little antique shop near the flat in Lexham Gardens where in 1955 I saw a gilt bronze Tibetan Buddha which I bought for £26 and which is now in the museum in Bath. I took it along to the Victoria & Albert Museum and asked if they could tell me anything more about it and they told me that it was nineteenth century (they were wrong – it was earlier) and translated the inscription as a form of blessing.

But what was most interesting about this piece was that it still had its contents and original sealed bottom. Most Buddhas have the bottom removed and the contents taken out but this one had not, which meant that it was still a Buddha that could be prayed to. The contents could be made up of many things, including filings of gold, iron and silver, and sometimes a smaller internal Buddha, made of gold or precious stone, and sometimes it was a sutra, a kind of prayer scroll. These contents could be quite valuable.

In July 1956, I completed my Articles and passed the Law Society exams and was admitted as a solicitor in the UK on 1st October, although by then I had already left the country. By that time, I knew I was going to return to Hong Kong but shortly before I was due to do so I fell ill with the flu. Aunt Flops decided I needed to take it easy and so suggested that I travel with my old friend Robin Fisher to Genoa, where I was due to catch the Lloyd Triestino ship *Asia* to travel on to the Far East. Robin had just qualified as a doctor and so was a good person to travel with should any further health problems occur and we spent a week before the ship sailed at Laigueglia, Liguria, near the French/Italian border, where I remember only that the beach wasn't very impressive.

But I was keen to be on my way. Following an interview with Anthony Lousada, senior partner of Stephenson, Harwood & Tatham I had a job set up, of which more in the next chapter, with their counterparts in Hong Kong, Johnson Stokes & Master, who were paying for my passage as they wanted me to get out to Hong Kong as soon as possible.

And so that slightly anxious week passed and I finally boarded the ship, en route to a place that since the 1949 Communist Party takeover of China had started to reinvent itself from a backwater to one of the world's great cities, helped in large part by the Chinese fleeing across the border. Many went to Taiwan but Hong Kong was also the destination for successful businessmen and entrepreneurs from Shanghai, people who were to contribute greatly to the colony's growth and who were already making quite an impact. Their presence was in fact one of the reasons that JSM wanted me to get there so quickly.

One of seven liners built by the première Italian shipbuilder Lloyd Triestino Societa di Navigazione, the *Asia* sailed during the golden age of sea travel, a comfortable ship equipped with living quarters, lounges, verandahs, card rooms, writing rooms and everything the discerning traveller could possibly ask for. The journey, which was the quickest way to get out to Hong

Kong at the time as it avoided the long passage down the Iberian peninsula, took a month, docking at Egypt, Aden (now Yemen), Pakistan, India, Ceylon as it then was, and Singapore. We also passed through the newly re-opened Suez Canal and as a result of the conflict there were still a number of wrecks clogging up the canal, a menace to shipping, but we steered our way safely through.

I arrived back in Hong Kong on 27th October 1956, the ship navigating mountainous seas which had been caused by a typhoon. We just caught the tail end of it, an omen, perhaps, of the tumultuous years that were to lie ahead. I also arrived directly on the back of the 1956 riots, the result of escalating tensions between pro-Nationalist and pro-Communist factions in Hong Kong. They resulted in 59 deaths, including a Swiss national, and compelled the British military to shore up the Hong Kong police before order was restored. This was possibly also a foretaste of what was to come.

When I got to Hong Kong I discovered that I had received another job offer, from Deacons, another of the major Hong Kong law firms. The letter offering me the post had been chasing me half way around the world and as a result the post offered went to Bill Turnbull, who went on to become senior partner, just as I was to do at JSM. And so the next great phase of my life began, and it was here that I was able to indulge in my two great passions: the practice of law and the collecting of Chinese art.

CHAPTER 6
IN AT THE DEEP END

I HAD ALWAYS KNOWN I was going to return to Hong Kong. It was where I had been born, it was where my father had spent his life and I always considered it to be home. In the event, Desmond did not follow on because he knew, he told me later, that if he too returned to Hong Kong he would never leave. But in my case, by now in my early twenties, I had decided that it was time to go and in addition to all that, I wanted to spend a bit more time with my father. I had seen him only intermittently during my childhood and now finally there was an opportunity to see something of him in the years before he retired, an event that was now on the horizon.

Coming home is exactly how it felt as I stepped off the boat and was met by my father to stay in his house. By now he was living in what was technically a bungalow at No 4 Black's Link, with a view out over Deep Water Bay, the beach and the golf course, but in reality the house clung to the hill around which it was built and you went up several steps to the bedrooms and down several steps to the servants' quarters. There was a small garden from which you could just catch a glimpse of the harbour. My father had bought the site from the government and after he had built the house, named it Tara after the Irish ballad "The Harp That Once

Through Tara's Halls". It was a beautiful house but it no longer exists. My father sold it for Canadian $65,000, a tiny fraction of what it would be worth today and another, much more ornate building now stands in its place.

Now I was back in Hong Kong and living with my father, as I did for the first six months I was there, he started to introduce me to all of his friends, many of whom held senior positions. Within the first few weeks I had joined the Jockey Club (a notoriously difficult place to infiltrate) largely due to the fact that my father attended most meetings as his firm were contracted to attend to any jockeys injured at the meetings. This was one of the first places where I came up against the then very rigid social structure in Hong Kong. On one occasion I was invited by Don Evans – Donald Brittan Evans, the senior partner when I arrived at JSM, who retired in 1961 – to his box and while there, the head of the enormous wine and spirit company Caldbeck Macgregor, Jack MacGregor and his wife Dot, the then arbiter of European society, swept in. Don attempted to introduce both me and one of JSM's assistants, Gareth Golby, who was also present at the time. Dot graciously acknowledged me on the grounds that she'd been at Roedean with my mother, but she refused point-blank to acknowledge Golby. I was very taken aback by her actions, although she was one of the last of a dying breed and Hong Kong was about to undergo a period of radical social change.

I also joined the Hong Kong Cricket Club, which was then at the back of the Supreme Court, now the Legislative Council building. With almost every junior expat a member, the Cricket Club was crucial for networking opportunities as well as relaxing in our spare time. It was also about a hundred yards from my new firm's offices and I was to lunch there almost every day. I first met Michael Stanley-Watts, a lifelong friend, at the Cricket Club, and his daughter Georgia became another of my godchildren.

COLLECTING CHINA

Me as a young solicitor

The Hong Kong that I was returning to was very different from the sleepy little backwater that I had left twenty years previously. There had been no building work during the war and many of the occupants had fled to escape the Japanese, but now the city had begun to change and grow in earnest as many people had returned. Since the Communists took over in mainland China in 1949, the Chinese had been flooding across the border, a process that continued throughout the 1950s and the infrastructure had to be built to accommodate them all. And so the three-storey buildings that had existed throughout the war were coming down to be replaced with taller buildings of twelve storeys or more, although unfortunately this did mean that most of the colonial villas that had characterised the city were also torn down.

And with this rapidly increasing population, Hong Kong had started to become an important manufacturing base. This growing sense of prosperity, for some people at least, was boosted by the fact that the British Government was one of the first to acknowledge the People's Republic of China – a sensible move, given its proximity to Hong Kong – which fostered a sense of stability. In the meantime, the Korean war made both the United States and China increasingly aware of Hong Kong's significance and its role as an import/export economy came to be of supreme importance. In the early 1950s, the textile industry started to develop and as the decade wore on manufacturing became more important, as Japanese products were going upmarket and something was needed to fill in at the lower end of the market. In the manufacture of cheap plastics, Hong Kong was ready to oblige. It also had the great advantage of being the only sheltered deep-water port in south China and had a railway system that could move imports and exports into and out of south China.

The Chinese believe that dragons hide in the mountains of Hong Kong Island. The dragon was beginning to stir.

When I decided that I was going to return to Hong Kong, I had contacted the two major firms of solicitors on the Island and they both made me offers. In the event, I decided to opt for Johnson Stokes & Master, a very well-regarded outfit that traced its origins to Edmund Sharp in 1863, which was now situated on the fourth floor of the Hongkong and Shanghai Bank Building. Even then, the whole building was air-conditioned, which made quite a difference in the hot and steamy Hong Kong summers.

Despite its stature, however, and a big shipping element which a similar firm in England would not have had, at that point JSM was essentially provincial in character and its own expansion was to mirror the explosion in economic and political significance on which it was based. Back then, we worked five-and-a-half days a week, with time off on Saturday afternoon and Sundays, and like most expats, including my father, we had contracts that kept us in Hong Kong for four years and then gave us six months off. I was to use these leaves to travel and see a great amount of the world.

But the business community of Hong Kong then could not compare to what it is now. In 1990, "Partners In Law", a book about Johnson Stokes & Master by Katherine Mattock was published and one of the firm's partners, John Gregory, summed it up: "There was no major banking industry, no major insurance industry. Nobody had heard of a merchant bank in Hong Kong. Land was HK$39 a square foot. There was only a handful of floated companies on the Hong Kong Stock Exchange." And, as the author pointed out, only half a dozen law firms – Brutton & Co, Deacons, Hastings & Co, JSM, Wilkinson & Grist and P. C. Woo & Co – featured in the Hong Kong section of the Law List and none of them had more than ten solicitors. That was about to change.

The day after I arrived in Hong Kong, I went to the office of JSM and reported to Ferdinand Gerald Nigel, who was then the second partner in the firm and subsequently became the Senior Partner from 1961-1971 until he was succeeded by me. The senior partner was Donald Brittan Evans and the other partners were Fenwick Deane Hammond and Harold Caine. I worked as an assistant to Nigel, as he was always called, drafting documents concerning wills, tenancy agreements and so forth, which would be sent to him for his approval, and as he was a good draftsman I learned a great deal from him. As with most European firms no one spoke Chinese so we employed four Chinese interpreters, who not only helped us by translating speech and documents but who would also introduce Chinese clients to the firm. They would receive a twenty percent commission on the fees paid by these Chinese clients, a system that over time was badly abused and was abolished by the Law Society by the late 1960s, by which time there were many more Chinese solicitors practising.

There were three other British expat assistants at the time: Chris Carr, who went on to marry a Chinese film star and was ultimately to leave JSM to start his own firm; Gareth Golby, who specialised in shipping cases and marine matters, and became a junior partner in 1964 before returning to the UK in 1965 when I bought out his partnership; and John Wilman, with whom I worked on minor litigation cases, and who was a great help to me in those early days when I was effectively expected to sink or swim. I swam. He left the firm some years later to join Judah and

Mike Watts

Randall of Kingston, Jamaica, but we stayed in touch and I visited him in Jamaica in 1965.

There were also a number of Chinese assistants: Frank Kwok, an elderly solicitor; Sydney Leong, whose family was of a rich property magnate; and Irene Ngan. Irene would pop in occasionally, having completed her Articles; her family were major shareholders in the China Motor Bus Company which held the franchise to run buses on Hong Kong Island. Irene was to play a significant role in my life, and was a recurring *leitmotif* throughout. After her father Ngan Shing Kwan, Irene was the most forceful member of the family, with her two brothers Henry and Horace generally deferring to her. She was a qualified solicitor but often, and sensibly, would ask advice of Leslie White while he was alive, one of the best barristers in Hong Kong and a board member of the family company.

Over the years I was to do a lot of work for the family, so I saw at first hand how Irene liked to operate. She didn't like paying for advice so instead she would invite me out for dinner, usually to a restaurant of which she was probably the landlord, bully them into producing the best available dishes, arrange to collect me at 7.30pm, actually collect me at 9pm, put me through the third degree over dinner on whatever subject was worrying her and then do exactly as she had intended all along. She used my input mainly to ensure she wasn't doing anything illegal and if I didn't come up with the goods straight away she would turn up at my apartment at 11pm and badger me until I finally managed to provide some advice just to get rid of her.

Although I had started work, I wasn't allowed to go to court until I was admitted to practise locally, but this was a mere formality which involved an application to the court where I had to appear in person to be sworn in and sign the roll, which was done in early January 1957. I was then allowed to attend District Court on behalf of the firm. I was thrown straight in at the deep end and my Articles had prepared me well. At that time, a system of "call-over" still existed in the Hong Kong District courts. Call-over was a very time consuming practice that had already been abandoned in the UK: it was used to progress District Court cases (Kowloon on Tuesday and Victoria on Friday) and meant that one solicitor from every firm involved in District Court cases listed that week had to go to the appropriate court once a week and wait – and it was often a lengthy wait – until that firm's list of cases came up for a hearing that would last a few seconds. It was so inefficient that rival firms would often ask each other's employees to stand in for them if they happened to be going to the relevant court. On occasion the long wait could prove useful, enabling both parties to come to a settlement.

As the most junior solicitor at JSM I was often sent to a call-over but once at the court solicitors were also called in order of seniority and as the most recently admitted solicitor in Hong Kong, I was the last in line there too. But this gave me the chance to watch my fellow solicitors and see how they performed. In some cases the performances were not very impressive: one solicitor burst into tears every time the judge ruled against her and there was another who kept issuing writs in the District Court which should have gone to the High Court. Years later I made notes about the performance of my fellow lawyers based on what I saw back then and passed these notes on to a friend, Richard Mills-Owens when he came to practise as a barrister in Hong Kong. He told me years later that I had got it spot on most of the time.

I was initially nervous dealing with these cases with other solicitors and the public looking on, but I soon got used to it and it was a good way of meeting my fellow lawyers and learning about their different competencies. Most of the solicitors were expats like me, using Chinese interpreters where necessary, who brought Chinese clients to the firm and received commissions for doing so. But this was yet another aspect of Hong Kong life that was to undergo a dramatic change. Over the years an increasing number of locals joined the profession and this turned into a flood when Hong Kong University opened a law faculty in 1974. One of JSM's interpreters was Liu Kwing Wah. I did a lot of work for his clients and he used me for landlord and tenant cases, in which I built up a certain expertise. Wills and conveyancing became my other specialities.

After six months my father set off on leave, the last before he was due to retire. He rented out his house so I looked for

COLLECTING CHINA

4 Black's Link, Hong Kong (Tara)

accommodation elsewhere. By this time I had managed to pass my driving test and had acquired my first car (a second-hand Morris Minor). I spent three months in a flat in Burnside, Repulse Bay before moving to the Lower Peak Tram Station, where my one-bedroom flat was on the first floor and where I could see the trams emerging from immediately underneath my bedroom. This is another Hong Kong landmark that has changed completely in the intervening years. In those days the building was only three storeys tall but has since been replaced by a 12-storey building and then again by a 24-storey edifice. By now I was earning HK$2,000 per month, of which the rent took HK$750, but I was doing well at the firm and was soon to see my salary rise. And I was able to start collecting, albeit on a very small scale.

I was also much happier than I had been in London: there was far more going on. I could play tennis and visit Hollywood Road and Cat Street, the two major streets in the antique district of Hong Kong. The countryside was also far more accessible than it had been in London. There is a commonly-held view that Hong Kong is an urban jungle with not a scrap of actual land left untouched, but this is far from being the case, even now. There were and are lovely countryside walks in Hong Kong, including around Black's Link, and these days the island is still home to several country parks. Hong Kong is so mountainous that some of the land simply can't be built on as it's too steep, which means that there is far more fresh air and wilderness than the Island is usually given credit for. And exactly the same could be said of the New Territories, just across the water.

I had inherited from my father when he left, a black Cocker Spaniel called Sammy, who accompanied me on these walks, and I frequently had the kind of adventures you could never have had back in the UK. On one occasion in my time there, I took a stroll around Sai Kung village in the New Territories, a settlement surrounded by sparsely-populated countryside, and bought a live green turtle, about nine inches long, in the Sai Kung fish market. I paid a local to row me out to one of the unpopulated islands in the bay, where I swam off the beach and released the turtle back into the sea, an idyllic scene the memory of which stays with me to this day.

Many of the villages in the New Territories had been abandoned in the 1950s and early 1960s because farming had become uneconomic and land values had risen. The farming families who had been born in Hong Kong all had British nationality and the right to full British passports, and most of them went to run and staff the Chinese restaurants then springing up all over the UK and Europe. During the Second World War and the Japanese occupation, the records of births, deaths and marriages were partially destroyed. The government had to do its best following the war to reconstruct them, which was fine if you had your original pre-war birth certificate. Alternatively, the midwife who attended your birth would hold this record. Rumour had it that midwives made a good living out of selling the blank pages of their books to people wishing to establish their place of birth and consequently their eligibility for a British passport.

My father told me about many other rackets appertaining to the Second World War too. On one occasion the United States raised a brigade of Chinese soldiers to fight the Japanese and after the war, to show their gratitude, they gave the soldiers, their wives and children American nationality and the right to live there. After a while the relevant authorities began to realise that the Chinese concerned were turning up an awful lot of children, an unlikely number in fact, and began to suspect that some kind of scam was going on. They thus employed my father to take blood tests to prove paternity and it soon emerged that the soldiers were indeed frequently not the real fathers, something that in no way put some enterprising souls off. One man turned up to my father's surgery with four children and when it emerged that two were not his, my father refused to issue the relevant certificate. The man concerned was a little put out but chalked it up to experience, and returned a few days later with another couple of children. My father refused to issue a certificate for them either.

The year 1958 was memorable for several reasons. For a start, JSM had been very pleased with me and gave me a pay rise of HK$600 month, part of which had been written into my contract and part of which was awarded on merit, which made quite a considerable difference to my lifestyle. I had some spare cash for the first time and I started buying the odd piece here and there, the first being an ivory goat with a kid at suck, which was probably from Nepal in the Himalayas and which I purchased for the princely sum of HK$80 (£5). Unfortunately, it was stolen from my house in 1997. I also began buying the odd bit of blue and white china, which is the route that many collectors start out on when they are interested in Chinese art, and this growing interest of mine became one of the things I had in common with someone who was to play a major part in my life in Hong Kong.

I first met Albert Sanguinetti at a party in November 1958 given by our family friend Jasmine Chan (later known as Jasmine Tyson), which he was attending with his friend the district judge Hugh Mills-Owens (father of Richard). Albert had arrived in the colony just a few days earlier from Gibraltar and was staying with the Mills-Owens family at the time, who he knew from his days in Kenya. Enormously flamboyant and with a personality that dominated every gathering, Albert, the scion of an old Gibraltar family, was a fascinating character, and totally unlike anyone else I had ever met. We formed a long-standing friendship that endured until Albert's death in 2009 and one of the many things that formed a bond was that we were both lawyers who were fascinated by collecting art.

And so we developed a routine: every Saturday, after working all morning, we would meet for lunch at the Cricket Club and then spend the afternoon on Hollywood Road and Cat Street, the antique centre of Hong Kong, pursuing our passion. Over time

With my step sister Liz Armour at Rannerdale in the mid 90s

our interests diverged as Albert became increasingly interested in the Japanese variety, but the passion for collecting remained the same and we saw a great deal of one another over the years that lay ahead.

My father had by this time retired and moved to Vancouver Island in British Columbia, off Canada's Pacific coast, and, having been a widower for 25 years, suddenly and unexpectedly remarried, although he had informed me of his decision before he left Hong Kong and swore me to secrecy. Desmond was living in Canada by that time, so he would have been told, too. My father had known Margaret Bruce Molson, née Mackenzie, since they had become friends when he was in Edinburgh, and had maintained that friendship ever since. She, too, was now a widow, having been married to William Hobart Molson, who had died in 1955. Madge, as she was known, also had two children, Liz Armour and Margaret Torray, It was a very happy second marriage and they were living in Lansdown Road in the island's capital, Victoria, where I would visit them regularly when I was on leave.

The seeds continued to be laid for the economic miracle that was Hong Kong, not least because on mainland China, Mao's Great Leap Forward programme and the collectivisation of farms was proving to be so disastrous that widespread famine was prompting refugees to flood across the border, averaging 25,000 a month but sometimes topping the 100,000 figure. These encompassed everyone from wealthy Shanghai industrialists to hundreds of thousands of labourers, who bolstered Hong Kong's capability as a manufacturing centre but who lived fairly miserable lives in cramped accommodation, chiefly in Government resettlement blocks on low wages, manning the factories that were now owned by the Shanghai entrepreneurs. Their plight was later to be highlighted by another friend, the social campaigner Elsie Elliot, of whom more anon. This necessitated a huge building programme on Hong Kong Island, Kowloon and in the New Territories, with formerly small villages seemingly turning into large towns overnight, and as the construction sector boomed, so too did the economy. It was a heady time.

Heady that is, except for the poor workers who were actually expected to live in the very basic accommodation they were getting in the huge new resettlement estates. Families of five were expected to live in tiny units of just 300 square feet at a rent of HK$14 a month. The Government was also encouraging private sector land developers, almost all of them Hong Kong Chinese, to develop pre-war buildings. In order to do this, the new owners had to pay compensation, which in turn the former tenants used to put down a deposit on a new-build flat.

Many of these refugees made good in Hong Kong's booming economy. I recall one chap who started life in Hong Kong with two Singer sewing machines, and ended up with two huge factories employing 6,000 people. At the same time, opportunities existed in firms like mine: one illiterate occupant of a resettlement block had her son articled to me and as he was underage at the time she had to sign for him, which she did by making a cross. He ended up as a partner of the firm.

Indeed, for those who were prepared to work this was an excellent time to move to Hong Kong. During all my time there, there was virtually no unemployment and although there was nothing like a jobseekers allowance or unemployment benefit, those prepared to put in the hours didn't need it. The government operated a policy of stable taxation and minimal interference with business which did a great deal to encourage entrepreneurs. There was no income or capital gains taxes as such. There were taxes on various classes of income such as salaries, business profits, property income and company profits but no tax on dividends. Foreign income earned by a company or business or by an

COLLECTING CHINA

Aunts Mary and Flops at Anne's wedding (1957)

individual was also not taxable. There were substantial personal allowances and the maximum tax take overall was limited to 15-17 percent during the whole time I was there. In practice, only about the top 10-20 percent of people paid tax at all and they raised more tax per head of population than in the UK as there were fewer deductions. There were death duties but only on assets in Hong Kong, so companies based in the colony were not used for holding foreign assets – British Virgin Island companies were generally used instead.

The Government was (and is) the largest landowner in Hong Kong and it used to sell off land for development annually, timing the release to support the market, depending on supply and predicted demand. The time delay from land sale to completed development could be anything from three to five years after the land sale and this is where the majority of the new developments came from.

I too had decided the time had come to buy an apartment and in 1961, I paid HK$150,000 for a three-bedroom apartment in a new block that was being developed by the Tyson family, and was due to be completed in 1964, the year I finally moved in. It was on Conduit Road, in the Mid-Levels on Hong Kong Island and in the early years afforded me a 180-degree view out over the harbour, although that was diminished over the years as increased building work reduced it to about a 30-degree view. Inside, I furnished it in the Chinese style: my collection was still extremely small but I had some pieces of Chinese furniture. This was the first home I owned myself.

In September 1960, my first four-year contract working for JSM came to an end and this marked another turning point because I had to decide whether or not my future lay in Hong Kong. If I was going to leave, now was the time to do so. But I had done very well at JSM and clearly had good prospects, on top of which the firm wanted me to stay. I was offered a second four-year contract and, on top of the HK$2,600 a month I was by then earning (plus annual increments of HK$100 per month), I was offered 2.5 percent of the firm's profits, which they said would equate to about HK$24,000 a year, almost doubling my salary. I accepted. I was also aware that Don Evans was retiring, and with only one other expat senior to me, and the elderly age profile of the other partners, my future looked extremely bright.

Before taking up that next contract, however, I was entitled to six months' fully paid leave and so I bought a round-the-world air ticket and set off on my travels, the first of several extended trips I was to make around the world. My first stop was Taiwan where I saw the National Palace Collection of Chinese Antiques in Taipei, and from there I travelled by bus to Hualien, along the east coast of Taiwan. The cliffs along the coast dropped about 1,000 feet to the sea. At one point the road had completely disappeared and a makeshift bridge had been made with planks to span the gap in the road. The bus of course, couldn't get across so the passengers, of which I was one, had to walk across these planks to board another bus for the second half of the journey.

From Hualien I took another bus on the Cross-Island Highway, which had been built through the gorges with great loss of human life. It opened to traffic on 1st November 1960 and I went through just two days later, on the 3rd November. The road was considered an engineering marvel at the time, given the difficult terrain it crossed. It weaves in and out of tunnels, with rather unnerving views of the rivers several hundred feet below.

From Taiwan, I went on to Tokyo and then Hawaii, where I visited Maui – in my opinion the loveliest of the Hawaiian islands I have visited – and from there to Vancouver, where Desmond was working as an accountant at Clarkson Gordon. I then went to visit my father and stepmother in Victoria. In advance of my arrival, my father sent me an extremely long letter telling me how to get to Victoria if the island was fog-bound, not least because his honeymoon had almost been ruined by fog problems. But in the event, not only were there no fog problems but I liked Victoria so much I considered retiring there myself.

After Victoria I flew to San Francisco and travelled on to Las Vegas, where I spent Christmas, and visited the Grand Canyon in Arizona. I celebrated New Year's Eve in New Orleans, where I very much enjoyed the jazz and the French Quarter, and embarked upon a trip around the Caribbean, starting in San Juan, the capital of Puerto Rico, and then on to Charlotte Amelie in the American Virgin Islands, and Antigua. I recall in Antigua a lift going up a hill to a restaurant and humming birds trying to steal sugar from the table. I then travelled on to St Kitts, Martinique, Guadaloupe, where there was some drama as a storm had wrecked St Lucia's runway – our next destination – and the scheduled carrier was unable to land. Another stranded passenger and I had to charter a plane to get there ourselves, and after a few days it was on to Grenada and Barbados. The Caribbean didn't impress me very much – after the elegance of Hawaii, it all felt a little sleazy.

I ended up in Barbados and flew to the UK, where I spent some time with Aunts Mary and Flops before returning to Hong Kong in March 1961 via Venice, Athens and a trip to the isle of Hydra. The journey had been interesting, but I'd had enough of being on holiday and was beginning to get a little bored. I was glad to return to my office, my routine and my life. But the 1960s were to prove a tumultuous decade for Hong Kong as its economic miracle, allied to its tendency for boom and bust began, while for my part, collecting was to become a central point of my life.

CHAPTER 7
Cat Street and Hollywood Road

As the 1960s got underway, there were to be seismic changes both in my own life and in the city in which I lived. When I returned to Hong Kong in March 1961 for my second four-year contract, it was to a city that was literally throwing off its shackles and starting anew: the flood of migrants from over the border with China, fleeing starvation and the consequences of the Great Leap Forward meant that housing remained at a premium and the old, pre-war buildings were being torn down while new 12-storey buildings were going up and new land was being released for development. These new constructions would in turn be torn down one day to make way for even taller skyscrapers, the glittering modern Hong Kong of today, all steel and glass and striking prosperity. But those precursors to the temples of success were not quite as comfortable and luxurious as their very modern counterparts: I still had no air conditioning as air conditioners cost the equivalent of a month's salary and so the sweltering and humid summer months remained something of an ordeal.

My father had left me his cocker spaniel Sammy, also known as Sambo, when he went to live in Canada and Sambo died of old age towards the end of 1962. Unfortunately he continued to make his presence felt. Desmond and his pregnant wife Wilma were making their way from Vancouver to the UK in October or November of that year and I let them have the run of my flat in the Lower Peak Tram station when they made a stopover in Hong Kong, while I went to stay with a friend. What I hadn't realised was that while Sammy was no longer with us, his fleas were and had managed to find their way into the bed, although everyone involved was very nice about it. Shortly afterwards, although not because of the fleas, I moved temporarily to a garden flat at 10 Wong Nei Chong Gap Road, which had a small garden that merged with the trees and undergrowth of the hillside at its outer border. I saw a stick insect and a praying mantis while I was there before moving into my flat at Rockymount, of which more below.

My career had been going from strength to strength and my second contract gave me 2.5 percent of the firm's profit, which towards the end of the contract was giving me HK$70,000 a year. This meant that life was becoming more comfortable in many other ways and for the first time I really was beginning to have the wherewithal to collect quite seriously. My weekend routines with Albert had become very established and were spent hunting for treasure as we both pursued our passion for collecting, although our tastes had by now diverged. We would work on Saturday morning and then meet for lunch and if I wasn't going to the races, then it was time for a renewal of the chase.

Cat Street was the original heart of the Hong Kong antique market – no one knows where the name originated, although it has been pointed out that "cat" is a Chinese term for the handler of stolen goods, while the thieves themselves were known as rats. At any rate, by this time the street was the epitome of respectability, as was Hollywood Road (named after the plants that lined the street, not the United States film industry) and Albert and I had become very well known to the local dealers, who would show us their wares. Collectors, both European and Chinese, would mingle on the street, where the emporia ranged from quite grand antique shops to little market stalls. Back then it did still have the aura of a street market and we would browse through what was on offer, always hopeful of finding a hidden treasure that had not been recognised as such by the dealers and always keen to see what they had managed to acquire from over the border in China and from their buying expeditions across the rest of the world. Hong Kong was very much the centre of the collecting world for Chinese art at this point and there was a palpable sense of excitement in the air as we sought out new pieces and compared our treasures.

It had become known that I did not bargain but equally I had an extremely good idea of what an item was worth and so the dealers tended to offer me a fair price. They knew I would walk away if the price was too high. I had bought my first piece back in London when I was doing my Articles but now my interest and knowledge was beginning to grow. I started, as many collectors of Chinese art do, with blue and white china, which is one of the easier areas to understand and thus a good starting point. The thrill of the chase never left me: when talking to my then colleagues in preparation for this book, many recalled me returning to the office and showing my latest acquisition with some degree of excitement. I would gloat over it for a while and then it would go into the growing collection in my flat and I would set out again in pursuit of the next. But I had yet to collect at the level I would in later years. I was still learning about the area, jades were difficult and bronzes were not at that stage available. However, I did buy one charming jade, that is now in the museum, of a monkey holding a peach, which was about HK$1,400, about the equivalent of £80.

Throughout my career I concentrated mainly on real estate, landlord and tenant matters, trusts, companies, estates and litigation and a little bit of banking but in those early days in Hong Kong I took on two serious criminal cases. It was just about

Desmond, Jessie Chan (standing), Veronica Tyson, Leslie Fox (standing), me and Wilma at The Hong Kong Club

the only time I ever did so, unlike Albert, who was a barrister specialising in criminal cases and criminal case appeals. There was no legal aid for criminal cases at the time, but for murder and manslaughter cases the High Court could assign a solicitor and barrister who were expected to work for free and would dole out a couple of cases to our firm each year. As a junior solicitor, I was the one assigned to the cases and was subjected to various gruesome pictures of stab wounds. In one case the accused was acquitted of murder but convicted of manslaughter, and in the other he got off completely as the jury thought that the hospital had been negligent because the victim who had been stabbed need not have died of his injuries.

I already knew most of the leading figures in Hong Kong and I also met most of the leading visitors, as well. One of these was Princess Pari Arfa, who was the widow of the head of the Iranian Air Force who had died in a crash. Albert knew her and asked me if I would help. She was in hospital where she was being treated for malaria. Even though my first sight of her was lying in a hospital bed with a fever of 104, she struck me immediately as one of the most beautiful women I have ever seen – dark, sultry and quite stunning. She asked me to look after her belongings and when I collected them I found them to include a handbag stuffed with large diamonds. Two weeks later, she had recovered and when she came to collect the bag, she assured me that should I ever visit Tehran she would make sure I was looked after.

Another case I was involved in at that time concerned the Chinese preoccupation with "face", a concept that is difficult for Westerners to understand but one which is extremely important in the Far East, relating to a person's reputation, prestige accorded to him and standing in the community. A Chinese entrepreneur called Keing Wu owned Hong Kong Optical, a chain of shops in the colony and one outlet was on Nathan Road, where he had a ground floor shop. As the lease was approaching an end he went to negotiate with the landlord, who attempted to double the rent from HK$50,000 to HK$100,000 a month, and when Keing Wu objected, he was thrown out of the office with a 'take it or leave it' ultimatum, as if he were a beggar. Keing Wu came to me and on the grounds that legally the landlord was required to give him six months' notice and had not done so, we managed to drag the proceedings out for a year, until finally the landlord was reduced to begging him to make a settlement. Thus Keing Wu, along with saving himself about HK$500,000, had retained his face.

Face came into play immediately afterwards, too, as he presented me with a gift of HK$2,000 on top of our firm's usual fees, by way of thanks. I was unsure what to do about this, and took him in to see F. G. Nigel, a partner in the firm, to explain why he wanted to give me this money. Once Keing Wu had explained, Nigel agreed, for to do otherwise would have involved loss of face for Keing Wu. As it happens, I very quickly found something to spend it on: during a trip to Macau, I saw a magnificent Kang couch and matching Kang table which I bought for HK$1,200. The couch was in very dark rose wood with key fret panels in boxwood surrounding *famille verte* porcelain tiles, decorated with flowers, four in the back and one in each of the arm panels. The matching table also had two *famille verte* tiles and the whole piece dated from the early 18th century.

It was enormous, but at that point so was my flat and so it settled in quite beautifully, although sadly, when I finally left Hong Kong nearly thirty years later, I had to sell it as it was just too big to fit in anywhere. I sold it for HK$120,000, a full hundred times what I had paid for it – I absolutely always loved getting a bargain. These days, you could probably add another nought to the price.

That was not the end of my dealings with Keing Wu, either. I later became a director of Hong Kong Optical, the smallest company to be listed on the Hong Kong Stock Exchange, and took a few shares in the company. Some years later it was taken over by Dickson Poon who, through his company Dickson Concepts, was to buy Harvey Nichols in London and who had the kind of personal charm and charisma that made the deal possible. Keing Wu was not the easiest man to deal with but was won over here.

By this time, from around the age of 29, my hair had already turned quite white but far from being concerned about premature greying, I soon realised that this gave me an advantage. I looked older than I really was and this of course inspired confidence among the clients as they didn't worry that they were in the hands of a callow youth. The Chinese revere age, unlike the youth-obsessed West, and so I never minded the physical onset of the ageing we must all endure. I also moved into my new home in Rockymount, where I was to stay until 1990 and had, at that time, an unparalleled view of Victoria Harbour. I decorated my flat with Chinese furniture and slowly but surely it began to fill up with antiques. It was a huge place, 2,500 square feet with three bedrooms: one was separated from the main living area by a wooden partition which could be rolled back so the room could serve as further living space, while the third bedroom was used as a storeroom to house my growing collection. By this time, I could also afford air conditioners, which I bought as soon as I moved in, for all three bedrooms.

Throughout my time in Hong Kong, I was very fortunate to be looked after by two Chinese amahs (Filipinos were becoming popular but I was glad to have the traditional original), the first of whom was Lam Choy Yen. She was married to the gardener of Dr Eberle, one of my father's partners, and she had looked after his wife. She was somewhat unusual in that she was married, because many Chinese amahs adopted that role as they had not been able to find a husband. The Chinese are keen on ritual, and so these unmarried amahs would actually undergo a ceremony, much like a wedding ceremony, in which they were formally accepted as perpetual spinsters. After they retired from service with the Eberles, the couple bought a flat in Tsuen Wan with the gratuity that Europeans traditionally gave their Chinese servants when they retired. Lam, who was originally from Shanghai, first came to work for me in 1957.

Her husband stayed in the flat they had bought together, but she lived in my flat full time and worked as my housekeeper and cook; I picked up all the expenses and from time to time during the well over twenty years she worked for me, she asked me to invest her savings for her. I did so and by the time she returned to Shanghai in 1983, well into her seventies and with the gratuity she had received from me, that amount had grown to at least HK$500,000 – just another example of the entrepreneurial attitude displayed by the Hong Kong Chinese that was doing so much to energise Hong Kong back then.

My second tour of duty came to an end and as Hong Kong

continued to grow and the manufacturing industries became more sophisticated, moving from the likes of textiles and plastic flowers to electronics and more, the time for my second six-month trip arose. I was happy and settled in Hong Kong but we worked very hard in those four-year stints, and so the time off was necessary to recuperate. My love of travel came second only to my love of collecting and so it was time to set off again, starting with a visit to my father and his second wife Madge. Whenever I had a longer leave I always visited my father now.

I flew to Victoria to meet up with them and then we set off down the Hood Canal to Seattle, where a bad Dungeness crab made me so ill I was laid up for the whole time we were there. I then travelled on by myself to Los Angeles where I stayed with James Legay McElney and his wife Ella at Glendale, who took me to the original Disneyland and gave me a tour of Hollywood, as you would expect. I went on to Mexico City and Kingston, Jamaica, where I was able to spend some time with John Wilman, who had helped me so much when I first went to Hong Kong, and his wife.

From there I travelled to Augusta, Georgia which, while famous for its golf course, had many family connections and personal resonances for me, as well. During the war many Americans sent food parcels to British families and Addie R. Barnes, a very distant relative on my paternal grandmother's side had generously done this for us. I was looked after by a good friend of hers and my father's, Tito Barrett, while I was there. I was also introduced to Annie Fargo, who was related to my forebears the Davisons, including great great uncle John Davison, who had died in Augusta in 1877.

During that visit to the States I saw my father's cousin Peggy Martin who lived close to Washington, and I also visited another of my father's cousins, Alice and her husband Harold V. Smith at their flat at 84 Gracie Square in New York. He was the head of the

COLLECTING CHINA

Home Insurance Company and he too was a collector of sorts – he had the autograph of every American president, which he kept on his bar.

On my way back to Hong Kong, I took in some parts of the Middle East. I started at Beirut, with a side trip to Byblos and from there to Amman, which allowed me to see Jerash, with its impressive Roman remains. At that point Jordan still controlled East Jerusalem and Bethlehem so I included those cities, too. From there I visited the rose red city of Petra, through the Siq that leads to the ancient city, approaching it on a donkey led by an Arab who assumed from my white hair that I must be about 60 years old.

After exploring this beautiful site, which had lain undiscovered for centuries after being an important focal point on the trade route of the ancient world, I returned through the Siq on foot, just as the light was beginning to fade, whereupon I heard the roar of a lion immediately behind me. I walked faster and faster, finally breaking into a run and arrived breathless and very unnerved back at the hotel. When I told the hotel staff why, they were very amused and explained it wasn't a lion but a roadrunner, which makes a noise like a lion's roar. That wasn't the only unnerving experience on that trip: when I flew from Amman back to Beirut, the plane took off – and then we heard that most terrifying of sounds, two of the plane's engines conking out. I am not a nervous traveller but that was the only time on my trips that I felt real fear, although we were able to return safely to Amman airport and finally continued our journey on a replacement plane.

I flew from Beirut to Tehran where Pari Arfa looked after me as beautifully as she had promised, although we got off to a tricky start, for after she waved cheerily at me through the glass as I was going through customs, one of the customs officers pulled me aside and forced me to undergo a strip search, the only time this has ever happened to me. Of course, they didn't find anything but it was an undignified experience and I had to regain my composure before continuing through and meeting up with Pari, who whisked me off to her beautiful home and showed me the sights – which included the Shah's jewels, kept in a bank box.

I then undertook another incredibly uncomfortable plane journey in a Dakota, which had formerly been used as a military aircraft, but the destination merited it: Isfahan, the magnificent city that is the home of mosques and madrasas decorated with beautiful ceramic tiles in turquoise and *café au lait* hues, with stunning gardens surrounding them, all dating back to c1600. The buildings I was to see later in Tashkent and Samarkand which also had ceramic tiles, but in their case, reproductions, could not compare. And from there it was back to Tehran and then on to Hong Kong, where life was about to move up a gear once more.

The city was as bustling and frenzied as ever on my return but now there was to be a change to my personal circumstances, as well. By 1965, the opportunity came for me to be made a partner. Don Evans had retired and Gareth Golby was by now a partner but increasing family problems meant that he decided to return to the UK. He owned a percentage of the firm which now came up for sale and I decided that the time was right to take it. I was able to afford to do so because not only had my own income risen exponentially since starting at the firm seven years previously, but I had also received an inheritance. Aunty Flops had died in February 1965 and my share of her estate amounted to about £9,000, in addition to some furniture and silver, while the share in the partnership was to cost me about £10,000. I was able to pay Gareth off within the year.

Hong Kong continued to bustle but now there came one of the periodic downturns that characterises any market that heats up too fast. In this case it involved real estate. The frenzied building programme that had begun to house the Chinese fleeing across the

Albert Sanguinetti

border had got out of hand and by late 1964 there was a downturn in the property market which caused a problem with some of the local Chinese banks. They had over-lent on the properties and by mid-1965 we were seeing a series of runs on banks. Some went under completely while others were subsumed by HSBC and Chartered Bank, which were actually doing very well out of the crisis. The Chinese would withdraw their money from Chinese banks and then deposit it in HSBC or Chartered, which would in turn lend it back to the Chinese banks against sub mortgages or debentures. This was very good for our own business as we represented HSBC and I was kept very busy on this work for some time.

But it totally changed the face of banking in Hong Kong and created an atmosphere of instability that was to be exacerbated during the forthcoming riots. Sir John Cowperthwaite, the Financial Secretary in the colony, refused all requests for compensation for depositors, and the Hang Seng Bank ended up as a subsidiary of HSBC. HSBC had also helped the Far East Bank by extending loans in the middle of the crisis, but these loans were ultimately taken over by First National Citibank, which enabled Deacon Chiu, the Shanghai-born entrepreneur who had initially founded the bank, to buy back control.

I first met Deacon Chiu around this time: one of the best known figures in the colony at the time, Deacon would lunch every day in the Hilton Grill, then one of the best restaurants in Hong Kong. He would invite me to lunch with him two or three times a year and was a veritable fount of gossip. On one occasion he pointed out a European who, he informed me, was about to be promoted to senior superintendent of police but that the appointment had not yet been made public. Extremely well-informed and with a network stretching throughout every government office in Hong Kong, Deacon always knew exactly what was going on.

Sir John Cowperthwaite was in many ways one of the architects of Hong Kong's growing success: he was the person who established the low tax open economy which existed until the handover in 1997, with a maximum tax rate of between 15 and 17 percent. He reduced estate duty to a maximum of 18 percent, down from 52 percent when I arrived and there was no capital gains tax, all of which worked to establish a booming economy. His policies were continued by his successors, Sir Philip Haddon-Cave and Sir John Bembridge, providing a stability that enabled businesses to plan ahead for years, in contrast to the constant changes made by Chancellors in the UK. Sir Philip's son Charles worked in my office for a couple of months in the late 1970s after leaving school to see whether he would like to practise law. He obviously did, and has gone on to become a judge of the High Court in England.

But Sir John's refusal to countenance any form of compensation in the wake of the run on the banks meant that there were considerable losses among the Chinese community and this set the backdrop for what was to happen next. The following year, the Star Ferry decided to double its prices, from five cents to ten cents on the lower deck and ten cents to twenty cents on the upper deck. This sparked fears among the Chinese community that the bus companies might do something similar and a night of rioting ensued up and down Nathan Road in Kowloon. And so it was that I made the acquaintance of another notable Hong Kong figure, whose reputation extended far beyond the colony and who remains a name to conjure to this day. She was Elsie Elliott, later known as Elsie Tu. Elsie was greatly concerned with the problems among the less well-off in Hong Kong and became a noted social campaigner and a thorn in the side of the government. And as the riots worsened in the next year or so, hers was a voice that was heard everywhere as she fought for the rights of the Hong Kong poor.

CHAPTER 8
Kwai Lo

As the firm continued to grow, reflecting the pace of change in the colony, it too began to take on a new face. Our major clients were HSBC, Swires and Shell, and given that they were expanding rapidly, we had to follow suit. Hong Kong was by now a major manufacturing centre, an increasingly important location for shipping and chartering and it was also increasingly easy to reach from other parts of the world.

The growth of air travel meant that far from the month-long journey I had had to make when I started at JSM, it was now possible to fly from the UK in about eleven-and-a-half hours. Around that time we also changed our working practices: rather than four years on and six months off, we switched to what is standard in Hong Kong today, six weeks' holiday a year. JSM also paid for an annual economy return flight to the UK for their qualified solicitors, although it was possible to put that towards a round-the-world ticket, with the traveller paying the balance.

The Chinese solicitors employed by the firm also received this perk and many of them took the opportunity to visit Japan or Australia. I strongly believe extending the same benefits to the Chinese solicitors is one reason why JSM was so successful in attracting and keeping the best qualified staff. In 1964 we had also become one of the first Hong Kong firms to install a photocopier, which might now seem a standard piece of office equipment, but was at the time the exciting face of new technology.

As the face of Hong Kong changed, so too did the firm's personnel. Don Evans, John Wilman and Chris Carr had all retired by the early 1960s but Brian Tisdall, who I knew from our schooldays together at Marlborough, had joined the firm, and his daughter Olivia was to become another of my godchildren. Although Brian had trained as a lawyer, there was always something about him of the frustrated journalist, which he put to good use courtesy of an English language paper of the day, the *Hong Kong Standard,* Hong Kong's first and only English language free newspaper. (It still exists today, now called *The Standard.*)

Brian wrote a satirical column for the paper called Tiger Talk, which featured among much else an imaginary character called Ng Ng Ng. It was required reading among the expat community at the time and was capable of ruffling some feathers. On one occasion it printed what had until then been a confidential circular sent out by Chief Justice Sir Michael Hogan as a result of a visiting French admiral telling him that fines for traffic offences were too low and magistrates were being told to increase them. This memo was leaked to Tiger Talk (the culprit was never found out – Albert was suspected but point blank denied it) and a satirical version printed that attributed the remarks to an Icelandic sanitary inspector rather than a French admiral.

This resulted in two outcomes. For a start, Albert refused to comply with the circular on the grounds that it should not have been kept secret. If the Chief Justice had wanted the fines to be raised, this should have been made the subject of a court decision, announced publicly by the appeal court. The resulting row led him to leave Government service. The second outcome was that the Chief Justice became something of a laughing stock, which did nothing to improve his already fraught relationship with Albert.

Just before Albert stopped working for the government, however, his connections allowed me to see a side of Hong Kong that was virtually unknown outside the colony and seen by very few people. It involved a trip to Kowloon Walled City and was one of the most memorable days of my life. Hong Kong was on the whole one of the safest cities in the world, with even minor crimes such as pickpocketing and bag-snatching kept to a minimum, but there was an exception to this rule and that was this small enclave near Kai Tak airport, which was lawless, dangerous and could only be visited with an armed police escort.

Kowloon Walled City had come about when the treaty granting the lease of the New Territories was drawn up, which contained a provision that preserved the Chinese magistrates' jurisdiction in that small plot of land. The magistrates died out in the early 1900s, the Chinese Imperial system collapsed in 1911 and no-one knew what to do about the area. As a result, anarchy prevailed. It was full of fugitives from colonial justice, crammed with structurally unsafe buildings all bursting with too many inhabitants, opium dens and unlicensed dentists. Everyone gave it a wide birth.

But of course people were very curious, and one day the Belgian consul Viscount Serge de Robiano asked Albert to arrange a visit, and escorted by armed police off we went one Saturday afternoon. We started by attending a performance of Swan Lake put on by a troupe of overweight Chinese dancers who more closely resembled elephants than they did swans, at Lai Chi Kok amusement park (owned by Deacon Chiu, he who knew everything about what was happening to everyone else in Hong Kong well before they did). The idea was to introduce the Chinese to this beautiful Western art form, but the result was an absolute parody.

From there, we got into a couple of cars and made our way to

Kowloon Walled City. We met the armed police escort at the gates of the city and walked up the main street, which was less than 100 yards long, hemmed in by two and three-storey buildings on either side, constructed with little regard to building regulations and containing quack dentists on one side and opium dens on the other.

We went into one of the dens, where the prone bodies of users were littered on the ground. We saw the body of one addict who had died but whose body was still on the floor and had been there for some time. It was a profoundly depressing sight and the first time I had seen a dead body outside a morgue and so we were all glad to get away. The problem continued for years, however, until in the mid-1980s it was agreed it should be taken over by the government, a project that was entirely financed by the government with no liability at all on the Chinese. The city was demolished, with nothing left to hint at the human misery that had once existed there. The area is now a park.

The fact that Albert was no longer working for the Government freed him to take on a case from us involving Elsie Elliott, who I was to encounter periodically during my decades in the colony and who died in December 2015 at the age of 102. Elsie was one of the great social campaigners in the colony. After spending time as a missionary in China, she moved to Hong Kong, where she became a member of the Urban Council, which at the time was the only democratic body to which people could be elected and thus the only place through which the public could protest and make their views known.

By the mid 1960s, tensions were running high in Hong Kong. The bank runs had left a lot of people worse off than they had been previously and the simmering anger experienced by many people in the colony needed an outlet. In 1966 they got it in the form of the Star Ferry riots, which lasted for several days and resulted in over 1,800 arrests and one fatality. Elsie was on the Transport Advisory Committee and hers was the only dissenting voice on the committee over the fare rise.

Elsie was always certain that corruption was everywhere in public life and in this case she may well have been right because it eventually became clear that the police tried to set her up to take the blame for the riots. When the government decided to set up a Commission of Enquiry into the riots under the chairmanship of Chief Justice Sir Michael Hogan, Elsie, on the verge of a visit to the UK to report on the matter, was told that some detectives were going to try to frame her in connection with the riots. She already knew and liked Albert, who was sympathetic to her concerns, and so she sent a somewhat emotional letter to him expressing fears of a "slaughter of the innocents", and adding that the police themselves had employed thugs to turn the demonstrations into a violent riot and they were now trying to pin the blame on her.

Albert brought Elsie's letter to JSM, and we – Albert, Brian Tisdall and I – discussed it. While we all agreed that she appeared overwrought, we decided it was desirable that she be represented before the Commission in her absence, and agreed to do this *pro bono*.

Brian Tisdall officially appointed Albert to take on the case and although we initially thought Elsie might be exaggerating, it is now almost certain that she was right. She volunteered to give information, barring the identity of the person who had told her about the police plot, and having hurried back from London she spoke at length at the enquiry. But because she refused to divulge that information about her informer, she was held in contempt of court. But the authorities were sufficiently concerned about the public reaction that they declined to imprison or fine her and announced they would send her to the bar of public opinion "for censure" (a decision that was widely mocked). The following year Elsie polled the highest number of votes to date in her re-election to the Urban Council.

I got to know Elsie through Albert, who was a member of the International Commission of Jurists, known as Justice, which decided to set up a branch in Hong Kong. Plans came to fruition in 1965 when Justice Alan Huggins (later Sir Alan), Brian Tisdall, Albert and I met in Huggins' chambers and the first thing we did was prepare a report on the desirability of Legal Aid in Hong Kong. The social tensions continued to increase in Hong Kong, with the Star Ferry turmoil and the riots coming the following year.

My acquaintance with Elsie deepened when Brian Tisdall worked on her case. Elsie ran something approximating to clinics to try to help the less well-off; I advised her on a number of landlord and tenant problems behind the scenes and I always found her to be a lovely woman, passionately interested in other people and always keen to help those less fortunate than herself. When I did some work on Albert's life story following his death in 2009 at the age of 86, I interviewed Elsie, by then known as Elsie Tu after her marriage to her second husband. Her concern for those less fortunate never waned.

One of the areas in which I did a lot of work for clients was as an executor, and one case that stands out in my memory is that of Vera Hope Dell'Oro. Vera must have been a great beauty in her youth but by the time I met her she was suffering from Paget's disease which causes the bones to become like India rubber and bend. Eventually they can become cancerous, which they did in her case, and Vera died in 1965. She had been living in a small property on Clearwater Bay Road near the junction with Fei Ngo Shan, housing a large community of cats and dogs which Vera asked to be put down after her death. It was a disagreeable task but I managed it.

However, what was to come was more problematic. Vera had

asked to be cremated and have her ashes scattered, combined with those of her mother, over the sea in Hong Kong waters. Vera's mother's ashes were kept on the mantelpiece in the drawing room, where they were briefly joined by Vera's, but we almost lost them when I appointed the auctioneer Lammert Brothers to sell the contents of the house and they inadvertently walked off with the urns containing the ashes. I managed to retrieve them but now there was the problem of how to scatter them as Vera desired. At the time, scattering ashes over water in Hong Kong would have been seen as very bad joss (luck) and so none of my staff were willing to help me and nor would anyone take me out on a boat to facilitate it. In the end, in despair, I took the night ferry to Macau and scattered the ashes from there. These days, however, attitudes have changed to the extent that there are now designated areas to scatter ashes, as we were to do with Albert several decades later.

Vera's estate was worth about £100,000, and involved a trip to Japan to sort out a deposit in a way that avoided costs or estate taxes; it was one of the few times I was called upon to travel abroad on client business. I stayed with Mike Watts when I was there, who had moved to Japan in 1960 and was to stay on for another twenty years. I visited Kyoto, where I admired the beautiful gardens, as well as took trips to Hiroshima and Beppu, where I bought a lovely Tsuba and a Korean Koryo dynasty celadon. As Vera had no relatives that she knew of, she left most of her estate to a cancer charity. However, she also remembered me in her will and left me a Japanese parquetry cupboard which I had admired on a visit to her house and £1,000 in cash. This I spent on two Persian rugs: a silk garden Qum and a Nain, which with at least 400 stitches per square inch, (which is how the quality of Persian rugs is measured), was of the finest being made in the 1960s.

On another visit to Kyoto on my 48th birthday (I was born in the year of the monkey so my 48th was my fourth monkey birthday), I found a wood sculpture with four monkeys peering out from holes in a mountain, the whole designed to fit on the top of an incense burner so that the perfume would waft out through the holes. I bought it as the coincidences were too great.

Being an executor could also give you an insight into the quirks of a person's character and it did here. I discovered that Vera had forged her own birth certificate to knock ten years off the age in her Australian passport.

I was also to act as the executor for a businessman called Franklin Ming Dong Tsu two decades later, but it was in the 1960s that I first made his acquaintance and all because of a row – that could have turned into an international dispute – over wigs. Franklin owned a firm which was later to be incorporated as R&D Products, which made wigs out of human hair and exported them, its chief market being the United States. The only problem was that after China sided with North Korea in the Korean War, the US had banned the importation of goods either made in China or containing content which originated in China, and the only two countries at that time that could supply the right type of hair for wig manufacture were Indonesia and China. Thus, of course, the only types of wigs that could be exported to the US were those that were made of Indonesian strands. Franklin, like everyone else who exported to the States was required to fill in extensive documentation swearing statutory declarations about the fact that although it was manufactured in Hong Kong, the actual hair used was not from China.

Unfortunately, someone smelled a rat. This someone was an official in the US consulate stationed in Hong Kong to monitor the proceedings and make sure that nothing of mainland Chinese origin entered the US. This same official noticed a marked discrepancy between the amount of Indonesian hair that entered Hong Kong and the amount that was registered as leaving it, and brought heavy pressure to bear on the Commerce & Industry Department of the Hong Kong government to investigate. Jimmy McGregor – later Sir James McGregor – was working in the section monitoring and running the comprehensive certificate system and set the wheels in motion. He authorised a raid on the Tsu factory where there were found a number of invoices for Chinese hair from a vendor who had mysteriously disappeared across the border to China by the time the discovery was made. Of course, there was no problem using Chinese hair in wigs sent anywhere else in the world but not to the US, and it was causing a good deal of embarrassment to the authorities as the whole affair was damaging Hong Kong's reputation and Jimmy would have been glad of the opportunity to bring this practice to an end.

Franklin was duly charged with making false declarations as to the origins of the hair used in his wigs destined for the United States and the case went to court. And it was a deadly serious situation: if he were found guilty, it would have had terrible repercussions on the Hong Kong wig industry, which at that point was a thriving business, contributing to the growing economic miracle, to say nothing of providing widespread employment.

I was introduced to Franklin by one of the Chinese executives at Shell, who asked me to act for him; I was given to understand that Franklin's family had been an agent for Shell in Shanghai. I instructed Albert to act in Franklin's case and the hearing took place in the Causeway Bay magistrate's court. Albert's innate theatricality stood him in good stead, as did his knowledge of the rules of evidence, and every time an invoice for Chinese hair was produced by the prosecution he objected on the grounds that the person who had issued the invoice should also have been in court to give evidence. The magistrate agreed.

The problem was that the issuer of the invoice had (fortunately for the defence) gone to China and thus was not available to give evidence, although if truth be told, even if they had managed to get her into court it is difficult to see how the Crown could have proved that the Chinese hair covered by the invoice was bound for the United States. After three days of trying in vain to get one invoice accepted in evidence, the Crown gave up and all charges were dropped. Franklin was discharged. He nudged me on the way out of court: "It's a pleasure to do business in a place where the rule of law is so strong," he said. Jimmy McGregor may not have been thrilled, but at least it got the Americans off his back. His career went from strength to strength in Hong Kong and he later received a knighthood. Meanwhile, stories circulated about one consignment of Indonesian hair which entered Victoria Harbour but, like some latter-day version of The Flying Dutchman of wigs, it was unloaded on paper and never in actual fact ever left the ship.

Franklin went on to become a very rich man. He had just been offered the agency for the sale of Kanekalon, a type of synthetic hair made in Japan, and I advised him to take it up. Chastened by what he knew very well was a lucky escape, he agreed. He thus took up the agency, used the new material in his own wigs and sold it to other wig makers (at a considerable mark-up). Kanekalon swiftly replaced the wigs made from human hair, Chinese or otherwise. R&D Products Limited, as he incorporated it in 1968 remained Franklin's major company until his death, and throughout the 1960s and 1970s, the wigs were extremely popular among American celebrities, for whom briefly it became a fashion to change their wigs as often as they did their dresses. Franklin made a fortune and forever after, he treated me as a lucky penny. I was to go on to do a great deal more for him, for after the fashion for wigs died down, he moved into real estate and made a fortune there, too. However, not content with the money he had already made, ultimately he was to overreach himself badly and in the wake of his death several decades hence, it was to take me a long time to untangle his affairs.

In March 1967, Fen Hammond and Harold Caine retired from JSM and Brian Tisdall, alongside Gregory and Bryson, became a partner. F. G. Nigel, the then senior partner at JSM had never put Tisdall under any pressure about his newspaper column, saying it had no bearing on his work as a lawyer, but was nonetheless extremely relieved that Brian gave it up when he became a partner. That was also the year the firm opened a second office, in Kowloon.

Following the run on the banks in 1965 and subsequent riots there was a short term collapse in Hong Kong's property prices. My flat, which I had bought for HK$150,000, for a time lost a third of its value, although it soon shot back up again. But despite the general instability in the colony's atmosphere the manufacturing industry continued to boom and my fortunes within the firm continued to rise. I rose to become second partner in 1967 and inherited Fen Hammond's office on the fourth floor of the HSBC building, about ten yards from a balcony on the Bank of China building, which afforded me a prime view of the demonstrations – as detailed in the first chapter of this book, the noise they made was not conducive to work. And I also inherited Betty Primrose, his secretary. Betty was to play a big role in my life from then on: an immensely capable woman, she ended up as office manager and was so efficient that when she retired, we had to hire five people to take over her role.

I also inherited some very interesting clients. Fen acted for the Chiap Hua group of companies, which had founded Eastern Time, a joint venture with Time Corporation in the United States. I became a director of Eastern Time, as well as another company in the group, International Containers, a joint venture between Chiap Hua and the Australian company Comalco which manufactured containers on Tsing Yi Island, off Tsuen Wan.

This appointment gave me fascinating insights into business and manufacturing that most lawyers would not normally have. My role was to ensure that the articles were followed and that the English-speaking half did not try to take advantage of the Chinese. It also afforded some travel and collecting opportunities over the course of time. In 1974 I was invited to join Cathay Pacific's inaugural non-stop flight from Hong Kong to Sydney, from where I travelled on to Melbourne, for an International Containers board meeting. I stayed in the Southern Cross Hotel, where I found in the curio shop one of my most significant purchases – a Northern Song jade fat-tailed sheep. The directors were also invited to visit Weipa on the Gulf of Carpentaria / Cape York Peninsula, where Comalco were mining bauxite. The six-hour flight from Melbourne to Cape York was made considerably more comfortable, not only because it took place on the company's private plane but also because I now had this beautiful piece to drool over.

The excitement of Hong Kong's growth was always offset by the instability that swelled into the rioting described in the first chapter, which couldn't help but impinge upon us, happy as I was with life otherwise. The acting Governor Sir Jack Cater continued to take a firm line and the Government pushed through a Public Order ordinance. This however turned out to be so badly drafted that it made the LegCo – the Legislative Council of Hong Kong – an illegal assembly: the draft bill made gatherings of five or more people in a public place an unlawful assembly; under other legislation the Legislative Council Chamber had been made a public place to enable residents to watch proceedings. Consequently when the LegCo met it was deemed an unlawful assembly. This Ordinance was severely criticised in many quarters, including by Albert, me and the whole of Justice, and it ended up being completely rewritten.

Receiving the Dr Ip Yee medal (for the second time) in 2012 from the President of the Oriental Ceramic Society of Hong Kong

COLLECTING CHINA

As the decade rolled on, my interest in Chinese art continued to strengthen and deepen, and in the late 1960s I was asked to join the Min Chiu Society, and also became one of the founders of the Oriental Ceramic Society of Hong Kong. The original Oriental Ceramic Society was founded in London in the 1930s by some famous collectors of Chinese art including Sir Percival David and George Eumorphopolos, which I had joined in 1960. I was one of the founders of the Oriental Ceramic Society of Hong Kong which was established in 1973, with similar objectives to the London society.

The Min Chiu Society was the senior Chinese collectors club in Hong Kong and had its own premises near Lee Gardens Hotel hosting regular lunches and dinners, where members would bring their latest acquisitions to show them off and to be judged, favourably or otherwise, by their peers. I was invited to one of the meetings in 1968 and took with me a Xuande mark and period Timurid tankard, a lovely piece with a clammy feel like orange skin, which I had just bought for HK$70,000, from Tai Sing in Hollywood Road. Unfortunately I couldn't actually afford to keep it as it was so expensive and had arranged to sell it on to the well-known London dealer Roger Bluett for HK$85,000. He was going to remit HK$70,000 straight to my account to cover my own expense and pay the rest when he collected the piece a week later.

Even so, there was still going to be a few days between the money leaving my account to pay for the piece and the funds coming in and so I had to rush to the bank to ask them to clear my cheque, which fortunately they agreed to do. Roger kept the remaining HK$15,000 in London, some of which I asked him to use to buy a Yung Cheng Imperial Doucai floral bowl, a Transitional blue and white vase, and a Swatow polychrome bowl. I subsequently discovered that the tankard had been offered to another member of the society for HK$40,000, but he had rejected it as being too expensive.

I took the piece to the Min Chiu Society and on the strength of my expertise in spotting this important piece I was made a member, the only active Kwai Lo (literally "ghost") in Hong Kong to do so as everyone else was Chinese, and indeed Chinese was the spoken language at the meetings, although the members spoke English too.

These were serious collectors and we took a great deal of joy in evaluating each other's pieces but it subsequently emerged that the society harked back to China's older customs, before Mao and his cronies took over, which I discovered when I took along a Daoist three-peaked wooden brush rest of a dark aromatic wood which I had bought for HK$400 in Cat Street. One of my fellow members was a Chinese artist called Harold Wong who ran Hanart, the best Chinese painting gallery in Hong Kong at the time, and he begged me to give him the brush rest, which I did as a gesture of friendship, as the mandarins of China would once have done. I didn't expect anything in return but a little while later he presented me with one of his Chinese landscape paintings, which would be worth quite a lot today. In future years, I gave this painting along with about 350 other works to the Art Gallery of Greater Victoria, which by now was looking after quite a bit of my own collection as I continued to send it out of the colony.

I lent pieces to every Min Chiu Society exhibition from 1968 to 1991, but by the 1970s there were sufficient numbers of fellow "kwai lo" collecting in Hong Kong, attracted by the growing internationalism of the colony, that we decided a society catering to our interests was needed as well. And so, in 1974, the Oriental Ceramic Society of Hong Kong was born. Founding members included such luminaries as Professor Brian Lofts of the University of Hong Kong and Duncan MacIntosh, an expert on blue and white porcelain, who were shortly afterwards joined by Dr Philip

Wen-Chee Mao, the society's first president, and of course me. I became the society's second president between 1977 and 1979, and was succeeded by another very distinguished collector, Dr Ip Yee.

The OCSHK held exhibitions with good quality catalogues, and I contributed to many of them: the exhibitions featured blue and white porcelain, the Yuan Evolution, Transitional wares and their forerunners, art from the Scholar's studio, Qing polychrome ceramics, export wares and South East Asian ceramics. The society also had a journal to which I contributed articles, including one on the origin and dating of foliated dragon decoration for the first issue. After Dr Ip Yee's death in 1984, the society decided to introduce a gold medal named after him for outstanding contributions to knowledge of Chinese art, and I was one of its first recipients. I suspect the society then went on to forget they had given me the award, because they did so again in 2012.

Napoleon mirror with eagle and ball

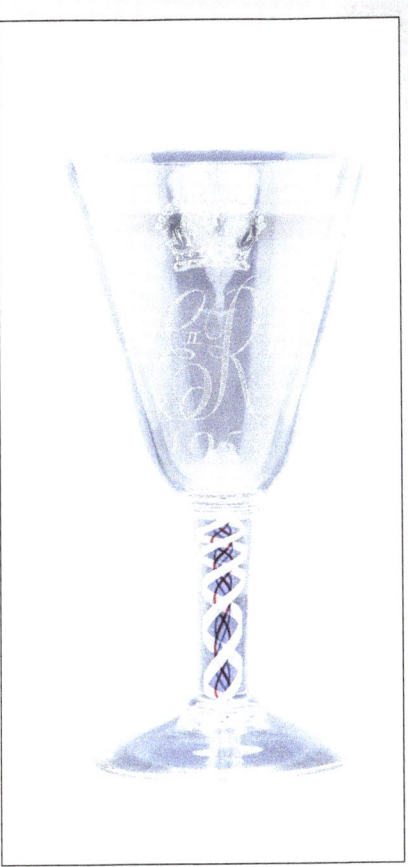

Coronation goblet

Ming ivory cane handle with Asian lion finial

Sino-Tibetan gilt brass Buddha

Blue and white early Kangxi beaker

Jade Bactrian camel

Blue and White transitional fish bowl

Bamboo carving of three frogs, dated 1623

Blue and white foliated dragon bowl

White nephrite jade bowl

Fat-tailed sheep in nephrite jade

Small yellow and green Yingzhong mark and period wine cup

Yongzhong famille rose brush pot

Yixing teapot by Yang Pengnian

Carved red lacquer saucer with Imperial dragon

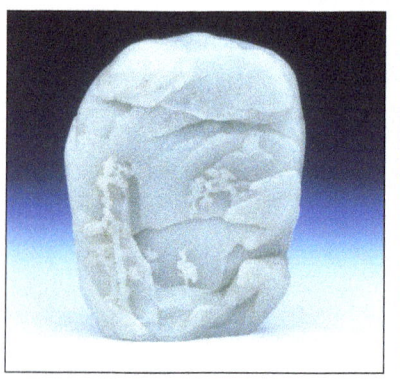
Carved celadon-coloured jade mountain

Hu Wenming-school incense burner with deer

Ordos standing bronze doe

Lead Bactrian camel from a Tang shrine c700 AD

Painting of Saanich farms by Colin Graham RCA (1915-2010)

George III silver tea caddy

Qingbai melon-shaped ewer with long spout

Five-lobed black lacquer dish with soapstone inlays

Blue and white tile with red underglaze c1670

Blue and white bowl with eagle on a branch

CHAPTER 9
SPIN THE WHEEL

AS THE ROLLERCOASTER soared upwards again, the recent riots and unrest began to show through in other, less expected ways. Many people had left the colony during the troubles which resulted in a severe skills shortage, and salaries nearly doubled within the space of a year for non-qualified staff. Inflation was soaring and the banking crisis meant that construction had briefly come to a halt, with the result that rents were shooting up, necessitating temporary legislation to halt the rise. I wrote a long Article on this legislation which was later incorporated into the syllabus of the University of Hong Kong's Faculty of Law, which opened in 1969. Subsequently, after taking a post-graduate certificate in law and serving Articles, the Law Faculty's graduates qualified as a solicitor, the first time it had been possible to do so in Hong Kong, which was the reason I had qualified in the UK. In fact, I had a close relationship with the faculty: I was made an honorary lecturer, and the major medal in the postgraduate exam is the Brian McElney gold medal in law, which I instituted to spread JSM's name among the students. While I myself didn't have a formal law degree, I acted for at least two years as an external examiner for the post-graduate certificate in law to ensure standards were maintained. (This proved, if nothing else, that a university degree isn't everything, at least in my case.) I also set papers for the accountant's qualification locally covering material such as fraudulent preference and the possibility of setting certain transactions aside in the case of bankruptcy or liquidation.

At JSM, meanwhile, we started a staff provident fund into which the firm paid five percent of salary. This did not cover the solicitors, but a rent allowance scheme was devised for them by Betty Primrose and her husband Robert, which either subsidised the rent they paid or allowed them to claim it against interest on a mortgage. This was a very clever scheme that worked as an incentive to keep staff on: during the 1960s and 1970s inflation soared in the colony, in large part down to the government financing its spending through land sales, and at the time I arrived most of the qualified staff were living in rented accommodation owned by wealthy Chinese. I was the first expat non-partner to buy my own flat but others followed suit, as did the incoming Chinese solicitors, and as rents rose this meant that our rival firms had to pay inflated salaries to accommodate their staff, whereas ours already either owned their own places or enjoyed lower historic rents.

Betty Primrose was by now office manager, in charge of the recruitment of all non-professional staff, travel arrangements and supply of office consumables among much else. Her husband, Robert William Primrose, always known as Prim, was also an important part of the running of the firm. He had retired from a job with the Hong Kong government at the age of fifty-five and we recruited him as the secretary to the partnership to help us implement our decisions and fulfill our duties. These included rotating our articled clerks, running our training programmes and allocating our resources and he was extremely efficient in keeping the firm ticking over smoothly.

In 1968 the Hong Kong property market took off again, slowly at first, but it soon began to escalate. An increasing number of banks began to be set up in the colony, marking the transition from manufacturing to financial centre and more family firms began to go public. It was also to herald the massive expansion of JSM.

In 1971, I became senior partner, a post I was to hold for twelve years, and the face of the firm began to change. I was joined by five other partners, including Peter Thompson and Michael Thornhill, along with eight assistant solicitors. The following year, in 1972, Charles Y. K. Lee became the first Chinese partner and Mildred Poon became the company's first female assistant solicitor; three years later, Betty became JSM's administrative manager. In 1974 we introduced mechanised accounting, just before the departure of our chief accountant Ebrahim Ali, who had taken on the monumental task of reconstructing our accounts from memory after the war, and the system went on to become fully computerised.

With the enormous growth in Hong Kong now very much under way again, we continued to have to adapt. We were facing competition from firms coming in from overseas, among them Slaughter & May and Linklaters & Paines, while the shipping scene had changed beyond compare. As one of the finest deep water harbours in the world and the chief entry point into southern China, Hong Kong was already extremely well-established when I first arrived, providing ship building and repair facilities, towage, salvage and docking, and all the major firms had ship owning or ship managing departments, and JSM had arguably the best legal practice in shipping and admiralty law – a specialised but crucial area – in the world.

I worked in this area only briefly in the early years. Nigel and Golby had been the experts in the firm, but when Golby went on leave I took over some of his responsibilities in protection and indemnity work. This covered cargo claims, workmen's compensation and accidents, not collisions or shipwrecks, and I checked and signed off the claims. I also boosted the mortgage documentation, suggesting amendments that the shipping lawyers did indeed take on.

In around 1968, having fulfilled the requirement of being a practising solicitor for at least ten years, I became a Notary Public for the colony of Hong Kong, an appointment that back then was made by the Archbishop of Canterbury. The number of Notaries Public in the colony was quite small in those days and entailed getting at least twenty sponsors, including the Chief Justice of Hong Kong, other notaries and prominent businessmen. The duties included witnessing the public signatures of documents and ensuring they were properly executed, having checked the identity of the person signing. These signed documents would henceforth be accepted almost everywhere in the world without further checking.

One of my duties as a notary, in the absence of other JSM notaries who were shipping experts, was to record "the protest" made by ship's captains; if there has been an incident during a voyage, anything from stormy seas to a potentially serious incident, the protest has to be made at the first port of call after the incident. The notary records it in a protest book under standardised language such as "fearing damage to ship or cargo" and can extend the description at a later date. It is important because this could form the basis of an insurance claim and equally could jeopardise a claim had the protest not been made.

By the late 1960s, Hong Kong was probably the most important centre for shipping in the world. One factor that drove it along was that the Japanese government was giving building subsidies to foreign owners building ships in Japan, but not to their own native ship owners. So Japanese companies would enlist Hong Kong owners to place an order for a new ship with a ship builder in Japan using a Liberian or Panamanian company as the nominal owner, which allowed the ship to fly the relevant flag and take advantage of those countries' slack rules and tax savings. It was then chartered to the Japanese company, which would pay the Hong Kong owner a hefty sum in return.

Many Hong Kong companies made huge amounts of money on the back of this, but at the time the colony did not have its own shipping register, or its own flags and regulations, which is why Liberian and Panamanian flags were used instead. However, as the 1970s progressed, JSM became increasingly involved in the development of the maritime register for the colony, with its own flag and regulations, all of which contributed to its growth as a financial centre (although older vessels retained the flags of other countries). Ship mortgage documents and banking agreements ran into seventy-plus pages, generating a huge amount of work.

The person primarily responsible for the work done in this field by JSM was Peter Thompson, who arrived in Hong Kong in 1964 and was himself to become senior partner from 1985-1989. Peter worked alongside John Payne in the firm's shipping department. Peter was appointed Chairman of the Hong Kong Port Development Board, which became the Hong Kong Port and Maritime Board, and created the first Hong Kong Shipping Registry.

I learned a good deal about shipping through the practices I encountered in Hong Kong too. One of the most extraordinary things I ever saw involved the chartering of vessels to transport salt in bulk from Western Australia to Japan. The way the salt was collected was to create a dam or lock across a bay and allow the shallow sea water to evaporate, leaving only the salt, which was harvested and poured into the chartered ship which then left for Japan. The sea was then let back into the bay and the process repeated. It was a tricky business because salt is corrosive, so if sea water got into the hold it could damage the ship – which often happened, causing any number of problems.

I was active outside the firm, too. In 1970 I was appointed a Justice of the Peace (unofficial), the duties of which included visiting a prison or correctional institution twice a year with an official JP to receive complaints from inmates and inspect the conditions in which they were kept. Usually we had to visit by helicopter as the buildings were so remote, but my general impression was that the prison service did an excellent job, dealing sensitively with the different racial groups, and providing education services to help the inmates on release, and we received very few complaints.

In 1971, I joined the Law Society Committee and was their representative on the legal aid advisory committee. I also became a member of the Board of Review, the initial fact-finding tribunal regarding tax appeals from the Commissioner of the Inland Revenue.

In 1973, I was elected president of the Hong Kong Law Society, and played a significant role in the growing internationalisation of the colony, especially as far as its growing reputation as a financial centre was concerned. During the rioting, some international banks such as First National City Bank (now Citibank) had moved out of the colony, but they now returned, accompanied by the others – Chase Manhattan, and many banks from Japan, Australia, Canada and the UK. Bankers need lawyers to advise them on whether their activities comply with the law of the country they are operating in and so where banks go, law firms will follow. There was some debate within the Hong Kong legal community as to whether these new firms of lawyers should be welcomed but I was very much of the opinion that they should be, as long as they didn't advise on deals that involved only Hong Kong law. The first of the foreign firms to arrive was Coudert Brothers, a Canadian company, which was no surprise as many wealthy Chinese had temporarily left the colony for Canada during the unrest and were now making their way back.

The boom was further fuelled by the fact that the government started investing heavily in infrastructure, matched by spending in the private sector. The government awarded a thirty-year franchise to build the first cross-harbour tunnel which opened in 1972, the first-ever road link between Hong Kong Island and Kowloon.

This enormous project needed financing and an application was made to the English export credit guarantee corporation for the necessary backing but they were turned down. The Chairman of the company, John Douglas Clague, seceded to appeal to the then UK prime minister Harold Wilson and having got an appointment, he flew to London with an assistant via Paris, where the assistant remained. Before Clague saw the PM he received a telex from his assistant to the effect that the French were offering French export credit financing as long as the company employed French contractors. This was reported to Harold Wilson who then rang the English export credit guarantee corporation and asked them to extend the credit required as long as the company employed English contractors. In consequence Costains built the tunnel with sterling funds borrowed at HK$16 = £1. The tunnel was completed in 1972 and the borrowings were repaid when the exchange rate had risen to HK$10 = £1. I believe that story is accurate but I was never able to ascertain whether the assistant ever saw the French export credit corporation; my guess is he did not, though the giant French construction company Dragages was then active in Hong Kong, which lent some credence to the telex. Douglas Clague was subsequently knighted.

At the same time the Swire group, which had had a presence in Hong Kong since the nineteenth century, began its development of the enormous dockyard site and adjoining properties at North

Point/Quarry Bay, which was so massive in scale that a virtual new town was being built on the island, known as Taikoo Shing. Work also started at this time on the Ocean Terminal in Kowloon.

I did a great deal of work on the Taikoo Shing development preparing all the documentation, and it became a model for other large-scale developments such as Discovery Bay on Lantau, for which I also prepared the initial documentation.

Meanwhile JSM was, quite literally, on the move. HSBC had decided to redevelop the building we had been housed in, which dated from before the war, and construct the gleaming edifice that is their home today. My office moved to New Henry House, but by this time the firm was expanding and it meant that other departments were forced to move elsewhere. Initially we couldn't find any other suitable premises to house the whole firm and so were scattered around the Island, but we ultimately ended up in four floors of Prince's Building, the largest tenants of Hong Kong Land, the premier office-owning landlord in Central.

One aspect of the rapid growth of the firm was that we started to form alliances with other law firms. This was continuing a process that had been going on in law firms in Hong Kong for a while. Two establishments called Hall Brutton, and Russ & Stewart had combined to form an outfit called Brutton & Stewart. In 1974, we amalgamated with them and in doing so acquired two very distinguished lawyers, John F. Payne and Robin S. Peard, both of whom became partners. Then in 1975 we amalgamated with David Burgin & Co, which had been operating since 1963 from premises in the same building as our office in Kowloon, and another respected lawyer, John A Mutimer, came on board as partner.

That year we also entered into a significant relationship with the London admiralty firm Norton, Rose, Botterell and Roche (now Norton Rose Fulbright) with some partners and assistant solicitors taking up residence in Hong Kong and working in our offices. I concluded the deal with them in a meeting in Athens, including a clause that they couldn't practise on their own in Hong Kong for three years after any separation. I also became a partner, although in name only, of their Jersey offshoot until my retirement. The accountancy firms on the island were doing the same thing: Price Waterhouse took over Lowe Bingham Matthews and Deloittes also took over a local firm.

I met almost all the major figures passing through Hong Kong in those years, and as the colony continued to prosper, more and more appeared. One of these was the entrepreneur Sir James Goldsmith, a charismatic character who held court at a private dinner in his suite at the Mandarin Hotel, regaling us with the gossip of the day. This was around the time of the Jeremy Thorpe scandal and he informed us that contrary to popular belief, about a third of MPs in the House of Commons were gay, although he thought Jeremy Thorpe had been framed. He took over a company on the Kowloon Exchange and announced it was going to be his personal investment vehicle and on the strength of that alone, I bought some shares in the company, which went on to do very well.

The stock market in Hong Kong at this point resembled nothing so much as a casino. The Chinese adore gambling and to them this was just another spin of the roulette wheel. The flood of flotations continued and it was not unusual for shares to rise to a 200 percent premium; in the meantime, of course, this created an enormous amount of work for JSM.

The international business community continued to beat its way to our doors. Malcolm Horsman, who had made millions with Slater Walker in the 1960s and 1970s and who became CEO of Bowaters Ralli arrived with his second in command, Alister Goodlad. The two of them took over Harry Odell Productions, which at the time was a tiny, moribund company quoted on the Hong Kong stock exchange, and through a rights issue and the takeover of various real estate companies, built it up into a giant and rechristened it Cathay Securities. It was all part of the rambunctious nature of the markets in those days: there were no insider dealing laws back then, no reporting requirements for buying and selling by directors and only a requirement to show directors' shareholdings in the annual report. There were fortunes to be made, although sellers of properties for shares usually had a clause prohibiting the sale of the shares for a period. Something similar was to happen in the dotcom boom of the 1990s, although by this time the regulations had changed and insider dealing had become a crime and directors' share dealings had to be reported at once.

Horsman did not actually stay on board for very long: Alistair Goodlad (now Lord Goodlad) took over and must have made a fortune himself. I was on Cathay's board for several years as well as that of Hong Kong Development, one of its publicly quoted subsidiaries, and was there when an old friend, David Kinloch (now Sir David Kinloch, Bart) took over the running of the company when Alistair left to stand for Parliament. In fact I signed David's application for UK citizenship for, despite being heir to one of the oldest baronetcies in Scotland, he, his father and grandfather had all been born outside the UK.

I also worked on the flotation of the real estate developer Great Eagle Holdings, the company controlled by the family of Lo Ying Shek, and was on the board from 1974 until 2006. Like Franklin Tsu, they treated me as a lucky penny as I won a significant case for them and gave them valuable advice over the building of the Great Eagle Centre. The government had auctioned off a valuable site on the waterfront and specified that any development would have to incorporate a pedestrian element. Under building ordnance regulations this provision would allow the developer to add extra floor area to whatever they were entitled to build under the conditions of sale.

Great Eagle bought the site and of course planned to use this additional space allowance but the government sought to deny them on the grounds that they were including the pedestrian element because they had to, not because they planned it voluntarily. Great Eagle came to us and the case went to court where the Privy Council ruled that the government was in the wrong and that if they had wanted to exclude the right to the additional allowance, then they should have spelled it out in the terms and conditions. We won the case, a victory that was worth at least HK$150 million, and cemented a working relationship that lasted for years.

There were less agreeable cases too, one of which dragged on for years. I acted for Mohans when they floated their real estate business, Mohans Property and Investments Ltd, but the timing was off as it was just at the end of the property boom and the share price collapsed. Obi Mohan, also known as Gobind, who ran the company, was a spoiled young man and tried to blame everyone else. It emerged that he'd borrowed heavily to boost the company's share price and when that failed, he started to sue everyone he could think of, including me, who he tried to sue for HK$80 million, alongside Peat Marwick and HSBC. I was defended by Richard Scott QC, who went on to become Lord Scott of Foscote and Lord of Appeal in Ordinary.

Obi's modus operandi was to substitute a fresh claim every time it became obvious that the initial one would fail, and in my case, one of the substitutions came after the expiry of limitation period. In such a case the court has the discretion to allow the charge and in this case they did, saying my shoulders were broad enough to bear the charge. This went on for a total of seven years until finally Obi substituted his latest charge for one claiming I had guaranteed the share price would rise to HK$3 per share, a claim so obviously ludicrous it was laughed out of court and the case finally came to an end. It was a relief when the burden eventually fell from my shoulders. Broad they might have been, but it had taken its toll.

The roulette wheel finally came to an abrupt halt and the stock market collapsed with OPEC's doubling of the oil price and continuing troubles in China in October 1973. The Hang Seng Index, which had been steadily rising since 1968 peaked at 1800 points early in the year, only to crash to 300 points later in the year. OPEC's actions led to the largest case I ever worked on when we acted for Shell against Hong Kong Electric, which we won with Sir Patrick Neill, later Lord Neill, Vice Chancellor of Oxford, as our counsel on the appeal.

The case involved a contract to supply fuel to the electric company's power stations for ten years starting on 1st April 1975 with the price of the oil to be determined by that quoted in the Persian Gulf at the start of the agreement, with subsequent adjustments up and down. The contract had been signed some six months before the first delivery was due and before OPEC doubled the price. The dispute revolved around whether the date of the agreement or the date of first delivery of fuel was the date from which adjustments to the price could be made. It was held on appeal that the date of the agreement was the relevant date and the amount involved ran into hundreds of millions.

At the time all this was going on, short selling – the practice of selling shares you did not own and then buying them when the price had fallen – was illegal but the wily gamblers in Hong Kong's stock market casino soon found a way to get round that, by borrowing stocks. It was rumoured that one bank nominee company was found out when it lent one client some holdings to sell short and was caught when another client, who actually owned the stocks, returned from a long trip and demanded the return of his share certificates. He had listed the numbers of the certificates he had left with the bank and was thus not going to be fooled by being given another share certificate. There was a terrible row, although it was all hushed up.

A client of mine was a victim of a similar questionable scheme and I had to step in to save her skin. She had been using a broking firm to gamble on the stock market with margin plays, using share transfers and certificates as security. My client was told that her shares had been sold out at the bottom of the market and that she owed nearly HK$100,000, a situation which put her into a suicidal depression not least as she was already mortgaged to the hilt and in fear of being sent to jail until her husband brought her in to see me. I tracked down copies of both the front and the back of the transfer forms and through the information inscribed on them discovered that her shares had not been sold at the bottom of the market as she had been told, but at the top, and far from owing nearly HK$100,000, she was actually due a huge amount. After this discovery I went through the rest of her portfolio and discovered she was owed a total of HK$6 million from a series of false trades, which I took to be a pretty good result. The greed these people showed was incredible – if they hadn't pressed for the sum that they falsely claimed she owed, they could never have been found out. They paid up immediately and I have often reflected that this was one of the most satisfying outcomes of my legal career. The wheel spun once more.

CHAPTER 10
SNAPSHOTS OF HONG KONG

RACING RUNS IN THE family. My father adored the horses and his firm were doctors to the Hong Kong Jockey Club and this fondness passed down to the next generation. I was elected to the Hong Kong Jockey Club within a few weeks of my arrival and by the early 1970s I had become one of the 200 voting members. I attended regularly and was active in the Club, which was one of the most powerful institutions in Hong Kong. The Chinese are inveterate gamblers but horse racing was the only legal way of doing so in the colony, making it so popular that the betting on every race exceeded an entire week's at Royal Ascot. The Club took part in good works too, however, and raised enormous amounts for charity.

Despite their love of racing, the Chinese cannot actually breed horses themselves because the nutrients in the grass are insufficient, which meant that they went to great lengths to acquire a good horse. In centuries past, tea travelled from China along the "Tea and Horse Road" either to Burma and on to India, or over the Tibetan Plateau to central Asia, to be traded for horses – so many pounds of tea being exchanged for a horse, the amount varying over the centuries.

More recently, horses were imported from Australia by air, and if members of the Jockey Club wanted to own their own horse, they would enter a ballot either individually or in a consortium. If successful, they paid a fixed price for the horse and for its expenses and if they were fortunate they would get a share of its winnings. The horse was stabled at the Club and its owner would choose from one of a number of resident trainers.

My father had owned a few horses both by himself and with a friend called Nordal Wallem, and his most successful, Beat That, won the P&O Cup in the early 1950s. His other horses rejoiced in the names Ninety-Nine, Century, Strabo and Mourne, and his racing colours were an emerald green jacket with black-and-white hooped sleeves and a black-and-green quartered hat. I carried on the family tradition – and its racing colours – and was successful twice in the Club ballots: my first horse was Black Bronze, which won the Jockey's Invitation Plate in 1976, at the time a prestigious race. The cost to me in those early days was not very great as all the races were handicapped, but as the horses improved in quality, it became a far more expensive game. My second horse sadly had to be destroyed after an accident.

I also had a horse in the UK, not least because my cousin Anne adored racing and we wanted to run a horse together. By the 1970s my income was such that I was able to afford a two-year old mare that we called Jade Ring, sired by Northern Dancer, and stabled and trained at Newmarket by James Toller, a friend of Anne's eldest son, Graham. Northern Dancer had sired many successful racers so Jade Ring was also an attractive breeding proposition and one of her offspring, Jalfrezi, won £44,000 as a three-year-old and was sold for £97,000, which covered all my costs in my career in racing in the UK, along with a few smaller sums from Jade Ring's other offspring.

When I first arrived in Hong Kong most of the senior positions in government and across the board in business were held by

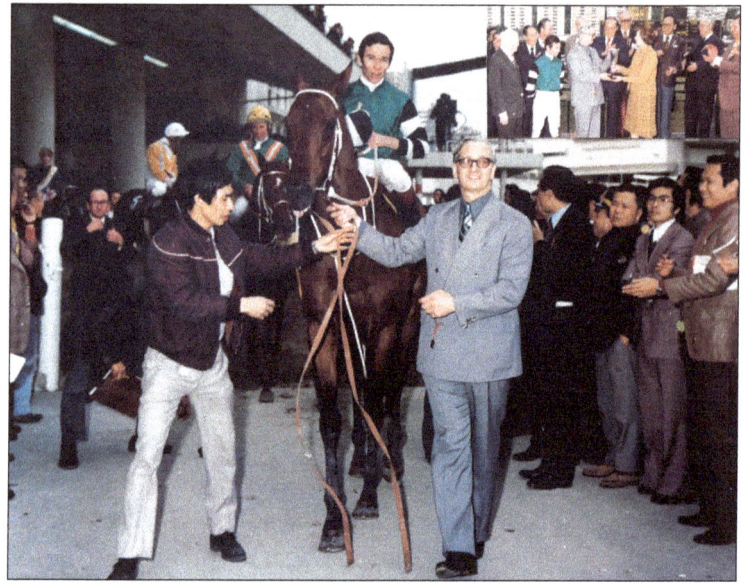

With Black Bronze after winning the Jockey's Invitation Plate, Hong Kong Jockey Club (1975)

British expats, although that began to change over time. What the British really did not understand, however, was the level of corruption to be found across Hong Kong society, although ironically it was one of their own who was to reveal the full extent of the problem and also to cause it to be addressed. "Tea money" or "lucky money" was demanded by officials throughout the colony, with even nurses and firemen demanding money to perform services for which they were supposedly salaried.

The expat community was very shocked by the case of Chief Superintendent Peter Godber: just before his retirement in 1973 it emerged that he held HK$4.3 million in various bank accounts, far more than a man of his rank and position could be expected to have. Confronted with this, he fled to Britain, using his police badge to bypass passport checks at the airport. But in 1974 he was arrested and extradited to Hong Kong. He was sent to trial, convicted of corruption and sentenced to four years in prison plus a financial confiscation, and such was the public outrage that Governor Murray MacLehose set up the Independent Commission Against Corruption, after which matters slowly started to improve – although an amnesty had to be declared across most of the police force for corruptions committed before 1975, such was police anger at the move.

This did not, it must be said, come as a complete surprise to me, not least as Albert had been a witness to the hard line police took with hawkers and had a good idea of the extent of the bribery that was going on. This was also confirmed elsewhere. At one point, the European Police Inspectors Association (in Hong Kong) petitioned for an increase in their basic pay as their lowest grade was below that of a police constable in the UK, despite the fact that the cost of living for Europeans was far higher in Hong Kong than it was back home. Despite this petition, their pay was not increased and when a few years later I asked a senior government servant why that was, he intimated to me that the government knew perfectly well that police officers made up their remuneration in other ways. And of course Elsie Elliott had also had experience of police corruption, receiving confirmation from the head of the Hawker Control Force some months after the riots that there was widespread corruption in its lower ranks (although denying that it had infected the inspectorate).

But it was in the temperament of the people to speculate and that included in areas that just tipped the border into legality as well. The massive building programme in the New Territories gave scope for huge potential profits, especially if you were aware of the areas in which the government intended to plan next, and family connections continued to be as important as ever when it came to finding out privileged information. The key was to become a "Letter B" holder: the government was buying up agricultural land in the colony for building and infrastructure purposes and would award a Letter B to the owner of the plot. Letter B owners were given the right to develop land elsewhere, a valuable commodity, and so there were many purchases of plots in the New Territories that were shortly afterwards sold on to the government in exchange for a Letter B. There was an active trade in Letter Bs and I once had a client who benefitted enormously from the situation. The government had bought up a large area to construct resettlement housing but failed to go through the proper legal process for one small area right in the middle of the proposed site. The owner of that plot consulted me and after I told him he could hold the entire development up for six months, the government suddenly became very reconciliatory towards him and awarded him a Letter B for the plot. He swapped this for another Letter B which entitled him to an industrial building lot and did very well out of the government's mistake.

Although corruption *per se* did not exist on the same level as it had done in previous times, the Chinese were never slow in coming up with any number of other wiles with which to protect their wealth. Inexplicably the government continued to impose death duties, which were utterly useless because they were so easy to avoid and very few people actually paid them. Duties were only paid on assets in Hong Kong, so it was extremely simple – and entirely legal – for a person to structure their affairs in such a way that a foreign entity owned their holdings in Hong Kong. I was once asked to draw up a will, one of very many I did for some of the most important people in Hong Kong, in which the testator left two percent of his estate in trust to help out indigent relatives (as defined by the Charities Act of Elizabeth I which applied in Hong Kong). The trust, which exists to this day, has never been able to find anyone who qualifies.

In such a rollercoaster of a place, with such huge amounts of wealth being bandied about, there was no shortage of interesting cases to become involved with. On one occasion I was called upon to represent the estate of a man who had died suddenly: he and his first wife had obtained a quickie divorce in Las Vegas and both remarried. The husband then died intestate and the first wife suddenly decided that the divorce must have been invalid and his fortune should go to her. The family came to me and I managed to find an authority from the Canadian Supreme Court which ruled that her remarriage after the quickie divorce acted as an Estoppal to her claim, which was consequently declared invalid.

On another occasion I was asked to make a case for change of an industrial site, on which a developer was entitled to erect a fifteen-storey building, into a container stuffing station on Tsing Yi island. The application was refused. I then discovered that I had made such a strong case against allowing the fifteen-storey building because of the effect on the infrastructure of the area, that the government offered the developer a change of use to commercial/residential use without asking him to pay a premium, which made the site far more valuable – and which I subsequently discovered was what the developer had really wanted all along. Even lawyers can be misled. The developer, meanwhile, made at least HK$100 million out of the deal.

Throughout all this time, indeed throughout my life, I was engaging in my two great passions outside work: travelling and collecting, frequently managing to combine the two. Living in Hong Kong, of course, I was able to travel all over the Far East, both for work and pleasure, as well as taking frequent trips back to Europe and Canada. Air travel made it possible in a way that could not have been imagined in my youth in the colony.

I often used to spend long weekends in the Philippines, especially in Manila, where I would explore the numerous antique shops filled with such treasures as ceramics from Vietnam, China and Thailand. At the time, explorers had recently found quite a few shipwrecks in the Pacific Ocean and ceramics seemed best able to survive the trauma, most of them blue and white pieces dating from the late 15th and early 16th century. As time went on and many other collectors also discovered that Manila was fertile hunting ground, prices went up and damaged pieces were repaired (sometimes clumsily) and sold as intact. As with all burgeoning markets, fakeries became a problem and you had to be constantly on guard against that. Indonesia was another great source of beautiful pieces from an earlier period – ceramics and celadons from the 13th and 14th centuries – and I visited in 1968 and 1972. Korea was another destination. On one of my trips to Thailand I was offered not only some beautiful antiques but also company, should I wish for it, to while away the evenings. I declined.

The flavour of collecting in Hong Kong was very much influenced by the influx of the wealthy from Shanghai in the 1950s and so it was Shanghai's taste in porcelain that predominated, not the Peking (now Beijing) taste in classic painting, bronzes and ink stones, although in the course of time I was to add all these to my collection. Even jades were subordinate to the interest in porcelain but, of the two, jades were the more important to Chinese culture. The actual centre of collecting Chinese art from 1949 to the end of the 1960s was London, dominated by Sotheby's and Christie's auction houses and backed up by respected dealers such as Bluetts, Sparks, and Spinks, but the emphasis was to shift to Hong Kong due to a number of circumstances.

The first was that towards the end of the 1960s, the price of Qing Imperial soared because one dealer, a Mrs Glatz, was buying on behalf of a number of Portuguese collectors, a situation which came to an abrupt halt with the overthrow of the Portuguese dictator Salazar in 1968. The prices of Qing Imperial collapsed and the ripples spread worldwide, affecting a number of London dealers who had been caught up in the boom and were now suffering.

Among them was a dealer called Hugh Moss, a great expert in snuff bottles, whose business had originated in London. He specialised in Qing Imperial ware and when the market ran into difficulties, he relocated to Hong Kong and sold off his London stock. His business prospered as he bought and sold all over the world. I bought several significant pieces from him from his ex-London stock as well as later acquisitions, such as the ceramic jardinière imitating pudding stone, the green robin's egg Qianlong vase, the pink soapstone figure, and the jade boy with black cat, all of which are now in the museum's collection.

Hong Kong became the undisputed centre for collecting Chinese art once the auction houses began to arrive. The enormously influential dealer and collector Robert Chang was one of those who persuaded Sotheby's to extend their business to the Far East, and in 1973 Sotheby's opened an office in Hong Kong. This not only brought even more collectable items to the colony but a great deal of expert knowledge, too. James Watt, who is now the Emeritus professor and Chinese expert at the Metropolitan Museum in New York, was there at the Hong Kong Museum of Art and acted as a go-between between the Shanghai collectors and the native Cantonese, who could barely understand one another. He and I were friends.

Christie's followed in 1976 and the presence of these two houses changed the collecting scene. They brought with them the traditions of Western auction house expertise to what had been a pretty subjective market, because until quite recently selling art had never held the kudos in Asia that it did in the West. The guarantees of authenticity, focus on genuinely good quality offers and the ability to give good advice changed the market, as did the presence of the highly respected Hugh Moss. The presence of someone who had been a top dealer in London who was now in Hong Kong served to focus attention on the East.

In the early seventies, several glossy magazines devoted to Asian art started to be published, and this further fueled the interest of the general public and collectors in the arts of Asia, most notably *Arts of Asia,* which developed a worldwide circulation.

I always had a jade in my pocket, and when I met James and other groups of collectors I would pass the jade round and we'd discuss it, not least as this was the time when an increasing amount of jade was coming in to the colony, most of it Han to post-Han, namely from about 206BC onwards, which would have come from tombs or personal collections where they would have been used as scroll weights. James occasionally recommended pieces to me if I bumped into him in Cat Street and went on to formulate a widely used system for dating jades.

By 1970, I had read and absorbed everything that had been written in English about Chinese ceramics and several of the books mentioned how rare and sought after Doucai chicken cups of the Chenghua period were from the time of their first manufacture around 1480. The Doucai palette is where the pattern is first outlined in underglaze blue, and the Imperial mark and sometimes borders are added and then fired at porcelain temperature of 1,200 degrees celsius. Polychrome enamels are carefully added to complete the design and then the piece is re-fired at about 600 degrees to fix the lovely translucent yellow, red and green enamels; purple enamels are occasionally included in the colour scheme.

Doucai went out of fashion shortly after the Chenghua reign but regained popularity in the early 18th century. In one of Sotheby's early Hong Kong sales there was on offer a Chenghua-marked chicken cup dating to the Kangxi period – around 1720 – and I managed to buy it for HK$40,000. The mainland Chinese had not yet entered the market and so didn't recognise the significance of the piece. It is an excellent copy of the original and in 2014 a genuine mark and period Chenghua chicken cup was sold in London in a once-in-a-generation sale for a world record price for any Chinese work of art.

In 1973 James Watt had been offered 1100 Lingnan school paintings for HK$250,000 and was given just two weeks to raise the funds. This proved to be all but impossible and he came to me practically in tears he was so distressed that he would not be able to buy the work. I told him that if he couldn't find the funds by the deadline I would give him the balance. It was this that finally prompted Mr Lai of Tai Sing dealers on Hollywood Road to get Chinese collectors to raise the money on the grounds that no "kwai lo" should be allowed to gift the money to a Chinese university to buy Chinese paintings. The money was duly raised, I didn't have to give anything and the collection, which would be worth millions today, was saved for Hong Kong.

All the dealers knew me and although they didn't contact me every time something new came in, often I would hear about a piece of particular interest to me and be told that the dealer had said, "Make sure this is offered to Brian."

I bought Song pieces dating from 960 to 1279, considered to be the third Chinese golden age, that came out of the tombs and as such were not of great interest to the Chinese, who were superstitious about this, and Chinese Qing porcelain, the last Imperial period, from 1644 onwards. It was not expensive back then, but there was not a lot of it about because those pieces were never buried in tombs and so much was lost or broken. However, I found a Tao Chai bowl with an Imperial Yongzheng mark, among other pieces.

As my knowledge grew, I continued to find beautiful objects in the most unusual places. I've already mentioned finding the fat-tailed sheep in a Melbourne hotel tourist shop, and equally surprisingly, on a visit to Florence I went into an antique shop and saw an old ashtray, which on closer inspection turned out to be an Imperial Ming lacquer piece and, I later discovered, one of only four known to exist in the world. I bought it on sight having realised that they had removed the fifth claw of the dragon in order to disguise the fact that it had probably been stolen from the Imperial Palace.

Treasures could turn up in the most extraordinary locations. Perhaps it is not so unlikely that a piece like that should turn up in Florence, one of the most sophisticated cities in the world, but Salt Lake City is another matter: even so, I found a lobed lacquer dish with soapstone inlays from the Kangxi period there at an antique fair, with a pre-war label on it from John Spark, one of the major London dealers.

Jades were coming onto the market in increasing numbers at that point and by the early 1970s onwards, the same could be said for bamboo carvings. I started to buy them as soon as they appeared in the colony and had two, dating from 1602 and 1623. As with so much else, once the Chinese realised there was interest from the West they made it their business to find increasing amounts and so they did, along with Han green wares, Neolithic pots and Liao ceramics, all of which had their own sudden increase in availability. Now, several decades later, all are far more widely appreciated and understood than they had been previously.

The Chinese dealers themselves were buying from everyone and another place they would source items was Japan. I had a number of favoured dealers: the main one was Leung Chai, a partnership run by K.Y. Ng and his brother-in-law. Another was Mr Lai from Tai Sing, a leading dealer on Hollywood Road next door to ManMo Temple, with whom I had a running battle: if he quoted what I thought was the right price I'd just sign a cheque, but if he got it wrong – too high – then I'd walk off. This actually meant that if he really wanted to make a sale the price he'd quote would be too low, but it suited both of us. It was he from whom in 1968 I bought a Xuande porcelain tankard in the shape of a traditional Timurid brass tankard. It was this piece that I took to my first meeting at the Min Chiu Society.

Another of the dealers with whom I dealt regularly was S.M. Chan, who had a small upstairs shop in Prince's Building, where my offices were, selling high quality expensive objects, and I bought half a dozen pieces from him. The other shop in that building was Galaxy, owned by B.K. Wong, which managed to acquire many very special pieces.

In 1974 a man called F.A. Nixon died and his effects were being sold by Lammert Brothers. I was aware that Nixon had given his Nestorian cross collection, probably one of the largest collections of such in the world, to the Fung Ping Shan Museum (now the Hong Kong University Museum), and I went to view the items in Lammerts thinking I might find more Nestorian crosses. Sure enough, I did but I also found an attaché case filled with old bronzes. I was in court on the day of the sale and asked Paul Mills-Owens (Richard's brother) to buy the two lots for me, the Nestorian crosses and "one lot of old bronze". When I came back at lunchtime Paul said "you didn't give me an upper limit, and I had to pay HK$4,000 for the Nestorian crosses, and HK$8,000 for the attaché case and its contents". Beyond thinking it of considerable interest I had not examined the case but when I did, I realised I'd got the bargain of a lifetime. There were 240 pieces of bronze dating from about 1000BC to 1000AD, mostly of Ordos-type material, and certainly worth several tens of thousands of pounds. I later discovered that many of the pieces in the attaché case had been exhibited in Stockholm in 1933 in the Hunting Magic Exhibition, the first seminal exhibition of Ordos bronzes.

With Hugh Mills-Owens and Albert Sanguinetti, Hong Kong Club

Originally called Sino-Siberian bronzes, they came to be known as Ordos bronzes after the area in which they were first found in the 1920s, a stretch of the Yellow River, and generally belonged to nomads who came from the steppes stretching from what is now Korea almost as far as the Urals.

The fact that the executor clearly didn't know what they were worried me because I thought that if I died suddenly, then my own executor might make the same mistake. And so in order to forestall that, I started making a catalogue, not only of the new pieces that I was buying but of everything I'd bought since arriving in Hong Kong. This was quite an undertaking because by now my collection contained about 500 pieces, although fortunately I could remember where I had bought most things.

Towards the end of the decade I branched out into a new area – 20th century Chinese watercolour painting, many of which were bought from either Leung Chai, or the previously mentioned Harold Wong's shop, Hanart.. Ultimately this collection contained works by 350 different artists and I gave it in its entirety to the Art

BRIAN MCELNEY

Gallery of Greater Victoria as a thank you for looking after my collection over the years.

In the 1970s I took two cruises with my father and Madge, and also went with them even earlier on a drive through British Columbia in early June when the Canadian wildlife are on the move after the spring thaw. We visited Banff, Lake Louise and Jasper. Our first cruise was on the *Pacific Princess*, which later appeared as the Love Boat in the television series of the same name. We started at Victoria and went through the inner passage to Skagway, Juneau and Katchican, with a side trip up the White Pass and Yukon railroad following the gold rush trail. The cruise went as far as Glacier Bay, Alaska where glaciers plunge into a fjord.

Jack in Jasper or Banff, 1976

Our second cruise, in 1976, was on the Union Castle ship sailing from Cape Town, where Madge had relatives, to Southampton. I stayed a few days in the excellent Mount Nelson Hotel, and visited Stellenbosch. The liner called in at the Canaries, the final passenger service plying the Southampton to Cape Town and back route.

In February 1977 I flew to Sydney for the Commonwealth Law Conference, and took the opportunity to visit the Hayman Islands, where Graham Fraser, Anne's son, and I took a day trip to the Great Barrier Reef. We walked on the reef, round a lagoon full of beautiful tropical fish but several of our co-travellers unwisely jumped into the lagoon to cool off and have a closer look at the fish, at which point a shark appeared and created absolute pandemonium as they all tried to get out again as quickly as possible.

COLLECTING CHINA

I also made a visit to a property I had bought sight-unseen several years previously, an old sheep shearers' bunkhouse in Toowoomba in the Darling Downs region of Queensland. I had bought it after frustratingly just missing out on a property in Hong Kong and I rented it out for nearly fifteen years. On this same trip I bought two more flats in the Potts Point area of Sydney, which I did see before I bought them. I sold all three properties when I moved back to the UK.

I also visited the Seychelles, during the 1970s, when it was still pristine. I took a boat to La Digue and bathed on its deserted pristine beach and saw a bird which at the time only had a few nesting pairs in the world. La Digue is now a popular resort and the bird is almost certainly extinct.

Visits by Westerners to China post-1949 were almost impossible. Apart from diplomats posted there the only Western visitors were those attending the trade fairs in Canton designed to bring together Chinese exporters and their customers. After the cultural revolution visits were still strictly controlled, well illustrated by the fact (to which I became privy) that Gough Whitlam, who had announced to the public in Australia that he was going to pay a visit to China, was refused a visa on the grounds he had not been invited. A friend of mine in Hong Kong saved his face and organised an invitation and visa for him.

In 1978 things were a lot easier, and I made the first of thirteen trips to China, at the invitation of Irene and Fritz Helmrich. Fritz worked in the trade section of the Austrian embassy in Peking, as it was then called. On my arrival he took me to a diplomatic reception at which everyone thought I was the new English ambassador; Fritz swiftly disabused them of this notion but I was pleased to be considered so quintessentially English. We toured the Forbidden City and the Great Wall of China, the first of several visits, and also some antique shops although I didn't buy anything then.

Anne, her son Nicholas and husband Denys Fraser

COLLECTING CHINA

I followed that with a visit the following year to Peking and Canton as part of a delegation from the Law Society of Hong Kong to the Chinese Minister of Justice. Representatives of all the major Hong Kong law firms were on the trip, but when we were ushered into his presence, the first thing he asked was who was the representative of Johnson Stokes & Master, and so I gained great face. It emerged that the firm had worked with him on a shipping case some years previously. We stopped off in a hotel in Canton on the way back but this was before China's hotels started to be brought up to international standards and I noticed that in the suggestions book, there were complaints about cockroaches on toothbrushes and a parade of rats running along the bedroom windowsill. Management didn't seem unduly concerned about us reading this, but then they wouldn't have been: the complaints were written in English and they wouldn't have been able to understand a word.

Another trip was with Anne and her husband Denys to Rome and Sicily in 1979. Denys returned to the UK early and we continued to tour Sicily staying at the Timeo Hotel in Toarmina, at the back of which is a well-preserved Greek theatre dating from about 400BC. The hotel afforded beautiful views of Mount Etna and we had hired a car when we arrived and drove along the north side of the island visiting the lovely towns and ending up in Palermo.

From there we went to Catania to catch the plane back to Rome and on to Heathrow. We were supposed to go straight from the airport to Graham's surprise 21st birthday party but when we called to find out where that was being held, we discovered that the party had been cancelled because Anne's mother Aunty Mary was extremely ill. We hired a car and drove straight to Anne's home but my aunt died before we got there. Aunty Mary was buried at Shenley Church, next door to their house. Her passing truly marked the end of an era, as she had played such a significant part in my upbringing and early life.

One of the most interesting trips I made was to Dunhuang, one of the major outposts on the Silk Road and famous for the nearby Mogao Caves, a complex of 492 temples. The journey, in 1982, was organised by the Oriental Ceramic Society of Hong Kong and my cousin Anne, her second son Martin and Paul Mills-Owens who happened to be in Hong Kong at the time, all joined the trip. We flew to Beijing where a sand storm was blowing but because it was mid-April the air conditioning in the hotel was switched off and our pleas to switch it on were unsuccessful. The heat was sweltering and we were not sorry to leave.

From Beijing, we flew to Lanzhou at the start of the Gansu corridor, another of the major stops on the Silk Road and visited the museum before catching the train to Dunhuang.

It was a 24-hour journey over mountain passes and across deserts with extremes of temperature on the way. The train went from the heat of Lanzhou over a pass at about 11,000 feet with temperatures close to freezing and we had to put on all the clothing we had with us in order not to freeze to death. Once through the mountains we spent hours following the extension of the Great Wall which was only a few feet high at that point, until we reached the Yumen gate (literally "jade gate") through which the Silk Road travellers passed as they left China.

Dunhuang is on the branch of the Silk Road which runs to the south of the Taklamakan desert (which in the local dialect is said to mean "he who enters does not come out") and is based in an oasis containing Crescent Lake and Mingsha Shan, literally the "singing sand mountains" which got their name from the sound of sand whipping off the dunes.

The railway did not go as far as Dunhuang and we had to take a three-hour coach ride from a station in the middle of the desert to the city, during which we saw a herd of antelope or gazelle and some camels. Once we got there we were put up in a reasonably comfortable hotel and the following day we were taken to the Mogao caverns. These caverns were carved out of the red sandstone cliffs by Buddhist travellers, who were pilgrims to the area, giving thanks for their passage and prayers for their onward journey. The caves were carved out between the fourth and fourteenth centuries AD when Buddhism was dominant in the region, and they are full of painted images and stucco figures of Buddhas, Bodhisattvas and Apsaras, donors and sponsors of the temples. Normally only two or three temples were open but the OCSHK had arranged for about twenty-five to be opened to us, at least one from each dynastic period so we could see the changes over the years. Climbing the hill behind the cavern were giant sand dunes and I picked up a pottery Tsa-tsa from the dried up river bed. Tsa-tsas were coarse molded depictions of many Buddhas in clay sold to pilgrims and merchants when the site was venerated.

From Dunhuang we travelled back to Lanzhou and flew on to Xi'an where we saw the Terracotta Warriors, the museum and other tombs. In Xi'an it was May Day (1st May), which is a public holiday in China, and our driver was so resentful of having to work that day that he staged a go-slow, allowing various ox carts to overtake us. Some of the party almost came to blows with him but I fortunately was able to smooth the situation and we managed to see all the sites and get back to the antique shop before it closed. In the various official antique shops on this trip I bought a number of significant pieces, including the lead Bactrian camel. As usual the non-ceramic items proved to be the real bargains.

We went on to Zhengzhou the following day and after a six-hour delay in the airport – during which I saw and bought a little gilt bronze dog, dating from the Tang dynasty – flew back to Canton, arriving there in the middle of the night and catching the train to Hong Kong in the morning. The plane ride from Zhengzhou was one of the worst I have ever taken, with one Chinese passenger going berserk after we landed in her attempt to get off the plane. We were all glad to get off the plane but it had been a fascinating trip.

CHAPTER 11
ALL CHANGE

BY THE START OF the 1980s, profound change was afoot, both in the colony in which I had now been living for over twenty years, and also in my own personal life. For a start, the status of Hong Kong itself was now coming into the international limelight. It might at one point have been possible to prolong the UK's lease on Hong Kong's New Territories, which was due to expire in 1997, but it was increasingly obvious that this was not going to be possible. In 1982 Margaret Thatcher, who had by then been prime minister of Britain for three years, flew to China to negotiate Hong Kong's future. Part of the programme included her launching a ship in Shanghai which I, along with about a hundred others, was invited to attend by the Worldwide Group which was controlled by the Hong Kong shipping billionaire Sir Y.K. Pao.

I flew out to Shanghai for the occasion and met the Iron Lady at a reception following the launch. When she established that I was a lawyer, she informed me that she did not understand the legal system in China, where the Communist party's dictats were effectively rubber stamped. I told her that the law was whatever the Communists wanted it to be at that time. That might have been an oversimplification but it was still very close to the truth.

The trip to Shanghai came in the wake of a couple of nasty

health scares, with something considerably worse still to come. I had a health check-up annually and in 1981 was informed that I was suffering from Type 2 diabetes. At the time it was not very well understood, however, and so I was advised to change my diet. Later on pills were added into the mix. Then the following year I had an attack of shingles on my face and while it was not a serious one, it was an early indication that the stress I was under was going to be too much to bear. And indeed, the day I returned from that trip to Shanghai, a lifetime of working very hard caught up with me and my health collapsed.

I had been planning on having dinner with a friend called Irene Ngan, who I mentioned in Chapter Six, and about half an hour after returning to my flat on the Sunday afternoon, Irene rang. I went to answer the phone but collapsed before I was able to pick it up. Fortunately my amah, Lam Choy Yen, was in the flat and hearing the telephone ringing came to answer it and found me prostrate on the floor. She picked up the phone and told Irene that I had collapsed and was unconscious. What Irene did next almost certainly saved my life. Her brother Henry was a professor of diagnostic radiology at the Queen Mary Hospital and lived nearby; she rang him immediately and he arrived within 15 minutes. He took one look at me and ordered an ambulance.

I came round as the ambulance men were bundling me on to a stretcher and established that I could still speak but there was a great deal of confusion as I was rushed to Canossa hospital, the closest to Rockymount. At first it was suspected that I might have had an aneurism, which would have required an operation but further investigations revealed that I had suffered a cerebro vascular accident. In other words, I had had a stroke. I was totally unconscious at the time but around me there was a hive of activity: Henry and Irene signed consent forms and guaranteed the medical bills; Betty Primrose informed everyone of what had happened

COLLECTING CHINA

and Desmond and my cousin Anne flew out to be with me. Neither of them left until I was out of intensive care. I have no recollection of events, but I was talking because afterwards Desmond told me that he invited me to visit him over Christmas in Tavistock, to which I apparently replied that I would have to think about it as I didn't know what his new wife's cooking was like. Apparently I also asked Anne after the welfare of her "crotchety old husband," something else I cannot recall, but my state of mind must have been obvious to everyone, not least because I am still on speaking terms with Desmond and Anne. I later discovered that I had been able to talk throughout, but I have no recollection of events from the ambulance arriving to waking up two weeks later.

I was in intensive care for a few days after which I was transferred to St Paul's in Causeway Bay, where I had been born. I soon regained full consciousness and could receive visitors, starting with Irene, whose chats could not have been good for my blood pressure as it quite frequently went through the roof. Anne and Desmond, meanwhile, saw that I was sufficiently well for them to be able to return to the UK.

Betty Primrose, of course, was a regular visitor and on one occasion she discovered me on the phone to my broker. I had now properly recovered consciousness and when I read in the paper that there had been a gas discovery off Hainan, I realised that the Hong Kong and China Gas Company would probably do well out of this, and got in touch with the broker to place an order for some shares. Betty later told me that when she saw this, she was confident that I would pull through. The shares I bought appreciated 1,000 percent over the next few years. Another visitor was Koo Yick Chan, one of the founders of Johnson Electric and later a major donor to the museum, who brought me shark's fin soup to help me to get better.

Even so, it was to take quite a while. After a couple of weeks, the hospital sent me home, but I needed a full time nurse and I was sleeping twelve hours a day. Eventually it was decided that I should spend some time in the UK and so Anne flew back to Hong Kong to help me on the journey, which in itself turned out to be an eventful one, as we flew back via Hawaii and Victoria BC. We had only just landed in Hawaii when a storm, Hurricane Iwa, hit the island and when we got to the Hilton it had suffered a power cut due to the ensuing storm. The hurricane also caused a tsunami, which damaged a nearby hotel so badly that the guests had to be evacuated and many were sent on to the Hilton, which meant there were so many guests the Hilton's staff and cooks could barely cope. I, meanwhile, slept calmly through it all.

We stopped in Victoria and saw my father and Madge before going on to the UK, where I saw a specialist who recommended that I undergo further tests as there was a possibility that the stroke had been caused by an hemangioma, something similar to an aneurism, for which I would have to undergo surgery. The result of the tests took about ten days to come through and during that time I took Desmond and his new wife Barbara on a cruise on the Nile to take my mind off it. In the event, an hemangioma was ruled out and no surgery was required. They came to the conclusion that the stroke had been caused by stress and overwork.

I was greatly relieved to learn that no operation was necessary but obviously there were to be some major changes in my life. The first was that it was not just I who had been somewhat traumatised by the ordeal, but Lam Choy Yen had been as well. She was by now in her eighties and told me that the shock of finding me unconscious had just been too much: she wanted to retire. She had saved a lot of money in the course of service with me and I had bought her a small flat for her retirement, but in the end she decided to return to Shanghai with her husband.

The ever-attentive Betty Primrose soon found a replacement

when I returned in 1983. Mak Mui, a Cantonese amah, stayed with me until 2007, living in Rockymount until 1991, and then at a place I bought in Chico Terrace, on Peel Street in Mid-Levels until I returned to the UK in 1992. Like so many of the Chinese at the time, she was financially very astute and had bought a share in an apartment in Kowloon, and she retired there in 2007. Her nephew, Mak Chun Chiu, had a very responsible job with the Hong Kong government, maintaining the mountainous slopes of the Island and monitoring for signs of landslides.

There also had to be some practical changes in the way I ran my life. After my stroke I employed a chauffeur, Ah Keung, because it had left me blind in the left eye, and with Hong Kong's heavy traffic and crowded streets I was likely to have or cause an accident. He would collect me in the morning and take me home in the afternoon, and if I was going out in the evenings he would look after me, working part time as a taxi driver when I was in the office. Like so many Chinese, he was a bit of a gambler. He played the market and eventually acquired his own taxi and a taxi licence which was worth a lot of money at the time.

The next great change was that I stepped down as senior partner of the firm, with (Thomas) John Gregory taking over, although I maintained a consultancy role for almost a decade after that. I had been senior partner for twelve years, and while on the whole it had entailed a great deal of hard work, it had also had its lighter moments. For example, in 1976, one of my partners, Robin Peard, asked me to stand in for his father Rear-Admiral Peard when he got married to a lovely girl from the Philippines called Vicky.

The ceremony took place in the beautiful San Agustin church in the Intramuros region of Manila. The ceremony, while an extremely happy occasion, was chaotic: hordes of photographers kept dragging cables everywhere and the Roman Catholic priest kept calling Robin "Robert." The ring got lost among the frills of the cushion and there was some frantic scrabbling when it was needed, and then Robin forgot to sign the register and had to retrace his footsteps for about fifty yards to do so. But everyone was in good humour and the subsequent reception was a lavish affair.

Being senior partner produced some moments of dark humour as well. I was once at a cocktail party when a man approached me, clearly under the impression that I had some control over my partners' out-of-work activities, although I was a little startled when he spoke. "My wife is probably in bed with one of your partners," he snapped. I was in fact often the last to know what my partners were doing outside the office: on one occasion I attended the second wedding of one of my partners, Mike Thornhill, at which the bride was clearly very heavily pregnant, something no one had warned me about. I was so taken aback when we were introduced I was nearly speechless.

I had seen a huge change in Hong Kong over the years, as well. In the early days I had visited the monastery at Ngong Ping on Lantau. Back then, it was really remote and one had to walk several miles up a private road built by Brook Bernacchi, a local QC whose father travelled with Scott to the Antarctic, to service his tea estate and farm on the plateau near the Buddhist monastery, with a walk from the plateau with its various nunneries, down to Tung Chung where there was an old fort, to catch the afternoon ferry. The monastery served vegetarian meals and this was a very pleasant excursion.

In the late sixties I had got to know Brook and was one of those he frequently invited to stay at his house and play croquet on his lawn. One Chinese New year, when traditionally new clothes are worn, I was dropped by the bus to walk the last couple of miles from the junction to Brook's house. I had arrived at the plateau when torrential rain started to fall and trying to find my way, I accidentally staggered into a paddy field, fell and ruined the new cashmere jacket I was wearing. It never recovered, but I made it to Brook's house looking like a drowned rat and had a bath immediately, borrowing something more suitable to wear instead.

On another occasion I was surprised that there were no eggs for breakfast because he had many chickens. Subsequently I was not so surprised that Brook had sacked his farm manager when he returned unexpectedly mid-week and found him selling his eggs and other produce in the local village market. Brook had a stroke and though he learned to speak again, his powers as a QC were sadly diminished. While he was recovering, his staff were using his jeep as a local taxi service. This came to light one day when it was left below the plateau and blown off the road into a ravine by a typhoon.

There had also been a lot of fascinating work. I have already mentioned some of my experiences as an executor: another notable one had taken place in 1974 and involved the estate of Roberta Marjorie Crerar Matheson. Marjorie, as she was always known, was the only daughter of a Hong Kong stockbroker who had lost everything in the 1929 crash, and at the outbreak of war in 1941 she was the housekeeper in charge of linen and room supplies at the Repulse Bay Hotel. Her Chinese staff adored her and the hotel was the scene of a major incident when it was taken over by the Japanese after an armed battle. In the aftermath, Marjorie wrote a report on the incident in which she commented on the *sang froid* of the Chinese staff.

Marjorie spent the war in Stanley camp with other British POWs and in the aftermath took a job as the manager of the Helena May Institute on Garden Road, but her health had been damaged during the war and she never totally recovered. The Helena May, named after a Governor's wife, was known as the Virgin's Retreat, as it had been established in the 1920s as a place of inexpensive accommodation for respectable unmarried girls who would flock to Hong Kong as part of the "fishing fleet", on the lookout for eligible men to marry. It was still being used as such, although in later years the fact that people now approached Hong Kong by air rather than ship meant that its character changed to become something more like a YWCA. Marjorie retired in 1967 and I helped her to find a small flat in Dina House and to invest the small lump sum she'd been given to fund her retirement, as well as assisting in other material ways. She was a remnant of another age but after her death in 1974, I found that she had not only appointed me as her sole executor but that she had left me a pair of emerald green jadeite discs which had belonged to her mother in more prosperous times, as well as a small Chinese carved table and some cut glass. The rest of the estate went to a cousin in Queensland, where her family had originated. It was Marjorie who introduced me to Johanna Austin, who featured significantly in my life when I returned to the UK.

The decrease in my workload meant that I was able to indulge my love of travel a great deal more and I continued to venture out with my cousin Anne. We travelled to Canada to see the Calgary stampede in mid-July in 1984, after which we travelled by coach to Lake Louise, Banff and Jasper, where it snowed despite the fact that it was the middle of the summer, and down eventually to Vancouver, seeing grizzly bears along the way. From there we went to Victoria and saw my father.

In January and February 1988, Anne and I met in India to view the wildlife. The tour took in the Taj Mahal and Agra, and Fatehpur Sikri to see the beautiful Mughal emperor's palace. We went on to the bird sanctuary at Bharatpur, seeing hundreds of different species of bird and a python, and stayed in a rather shabby hotel. While we were having a drink on the veranda, we noticed a man who was eating a curry on a low table about twenty feet away, who was called away to answer the phone. In his absence a jackal appeared from just below the veranda and started to devour the curry. The man reappeared, and the jackal vanished.

From Bharatpur we went to the Ran of Kutch where the party stayed with Raj Kumar, one of the leading wildlife experts in India, at his grand hilltop home furnished in the style of the 1890s, including a print by the English painter Herbert Dicksee – my grandmother had a print by the same artist in the Hill in Downpatrick. We saw bats in the tower and a bird of prey nesting on the roof, and in the nearby inlet, there were pelicans and guar, the Indian buffalo.

One day we went to lunch with an hereditary Hindu saint who, because of this status was a charity and entitled to tax exemptions. He also apparently was entitled to nominate his successor as the next hereditary saint. He had a string of rare breed horses with ears that turned inwards and curled at the top. When we arrived we were handed five pages of typescript detailing how his ancestors had become hereditary saints – seemingly by ensuring the rajah had issue.

Lunch was a bowl of yogurt and the men were seated at a table but women were expected to squat on the floor. I ate my yogurt but Anne noticed three bluebottles in hers and declined. When she put her hand over the bowl to decline a second helping, the servants poured the second helping over her hand. Perhaps unsurprisingly, members of the party had tummy upsets after this meal. During the meal, various villagers came to receive donations of food and to kiss the saint's foot, and when our coach left it disturbed a party of wild boar who were roaming the village streets eating the rubbish scattered all around.

From the Ran of Kutch we went to Bombay and after taking in the sights caught the train to Nagpur for an overnight stop. The following morning we were driven to Kipling Camp in a national

BRIAN MCELNEY

With Anne at Bharatpur (February 1988)

park run by Douglas Wright, who bore an uncanny resemblance to my father, and who had devoted his life to saving the tiger in India. We were at the camp for about five days, and every day we went out on an elephant trying to get a glimpse of a tiger in the wild: on the final day we saw a tigress and two cubs. Tigers never attack elephants and elephants can walk through the densest jungle, so you are safe so long as you remain on the elephant. We saw many other animals on our treks.

I was lucky enough to see tigers again when I visited Nepal in 1996. I did not go far from the capital, Kathmandu but I did get to the Chitral National Park where I was able to pat a baby Asian rhino and baby leopards and camped overlooking a pool with elephants bathing and Asian rhino close by. One day we were taken by boat on a river trip to see the gharial, a fish-eating crocodile. But the highlight was a tiger bathing in the river a few yards from us. It got out of the river stared at us and then disappeared. The guides told us it was the best tiger sighting that year – but my camera wouldn't work.

On another occasion, I joined a cruise from Akaba on the Sinai Peninsula with Anne and Denys, which went through the Suez Canal to Tel Aviv and on to Ephesus, Troy and Thessalonika, where I saw the probable treasure of Philip of Macedon, Alexander the Great's father. We skirted Mount Athos on our way to Meteora, and then went on to Athens via Delos and Mykonos, visited Crete and Majorca, and travelled from Gibraltar to Southampton with force eight gales blowing in the Bay of Biscay.

Another trip with Anne was to Morocco in a party of only eight led by Martin Jacoby, an excellent guide who, besides driving the vehicle, also provided a commentary on the flora and fauna, and at the end of the day provided computer printouts of all he had drawn our attention to that day. We started and ended at Marrakesh, and the end of Ramadan coincided with the last day of the tour. We got as far as the Sahara and a signpost to Timbuktu and we also visited the Summer Palace of the last Sultan of Marrakesh, which I found totally over the top, with dungeons where his opponents were no doubt disposed of. I began to have problems walking uphill and realised something was amiss – shortly afterwards I had my first angioplasty.

Now that I was stepping down as senior partner, I was to become the executor of another estate, except in this case it turned out to be remarkably close to a full time job. My old friend Franklin Tsu, he who had made a fortune from wigs, died in December 1983, fourteen months after my stroke. I was working during the mornings at JSM as a consultant, but if truth be told, I was becoming a little bored and welcomed a distraction, which this certainly turned out to be.

In the wake of making a fortune from his wig empire, Franklin had become involved in the manufacture of leather coats as well as real estate development and it was the latter that would have brought him down had he lived to tell the tale. He had decided in the late 1970s to get involved with a development in the Salt Lake area of the suburbs of Honolulu involving a forty-storey building with 160 apartments. He finished the development before he died and sold me one of the apartments at what he insisted was a "specially cheap price" – only for me to discover when I became the executor of his will that I had in fact paid the highest price of any in the development.

Franklin was suffering from type 2 diabetes and was nearly blind when he died of a heart attack. Diabetes was not very well understood back then and its longer term complications were not well known but the fact is that someone in Franklin's state of health should never have got involved in such an enormous project, which not only nearly bankrupted him but which put him under such great stress that it was probably a contributory factor to his heart attack. I flew out to Honolulu for the funeral and to meet his family before I was tasked with settling the estate. It was a very complicated case: before he died his wife had been suing him for divorce, a son was suing him for a great deal more and the estate was only worth about US$500,000 net. I was still working mornings only and in the event it was to take me four or five years in total, such was the complexity involved. I very soon realised that I was running his business empire, which had narrowly avoided bankruptcy only because exchange rates moved in his favour. Most of his assets were denominated in US dollars, but his liabilities owing on the Honolulu development were in Hong Kong dollars and so I found myself in charge of forty employees, most in the wig and leather garment trade.

Apart from the Hawaiian property, Franklin's other major asset was the wig building factory in Kwai Chung, Hong Kong. There were two potential purchasers and in the end I was able to sell it for a US$1million more than anyone had expected. The building was actually the subject of a specific legacy in the will: Franklin wanted the property to be sold and the proceeds invested to provide an income for his widow, concubine, and children, and a certain amount to go to charity. After his widow's death, the fund was to be distributed among the legatees, with the widow's portion going to charities to be decided by me, but including specifically museums.

In the event, because the estate was riddled with debt, it was agreed that the debts be paid out of the legacy, with the inheritors still getting a certain amount and the charities also benefitting. I ran the trust that was set up to deal with it all until Franklin's widow died in 1989, and when the monies were distributed, there was a net US$10 million, of which $6 million went to the family and $4 million to charities.

While I was working on the accounts, I took a cruise across the

Pacific and would fax the changes through to the office. Halfway through the cruise the work was complete and signed off and the final accounts distributed to the family. After a few days in Victoria, I went to New York to meet the family beneficiaries who were very pleased with the way it had turned out.

Franklin was by no means the only person I knew who had concubines: it was a common practice at the time. Another person who did so, and who was one of the most interesting people I met in Hong Kong, was K.C. Jay, who had been the manager of the Bank of China under both nationalist and communist rule and had been a friend of Zhou Enlai. He died as I was recovering from my stroke, another change in the Hong Kong I had known. I met him in the 1970s and established he was married to a lady who was blind and who I never met, and with whom he had eleven children. There were ten boys and one girl, who had been given the name Juliana, so that if and when she married she would still be a Jay. The boys, meanwhile, had been named in alphabetical order, presumably so that they would know their place in the pecking order.

KC was retired from the Bank of China by the time I met him but he was the head of the Foreign Exchange Brokers Association, and was the broker who did much of China's foreign exchange transactions at the time, and his office was in the same building as mine. His office was run by his concubines, Edna and Irene, and during our numerous lunches, frequently at restaurants in which he had an interest, he would regale me with stories about Hong Kong tycoons and their lurid pasts. These also often involved mistresses, one in particular being about smuggling heavy-duty tires to China at the height of the Korean war. The chief of the smugglers and the head of customs shared a mistress so the former got advance warning of any customs raids and shared the subsequent reward with the lucky lady.

COLLECTING CHINA

The US contingent - Kirk McElney, Robert McElney, his son Marc, James Legay McElney and me (California 1984)

KC was a man of many interests. His large house contained numerous breeds of dog as he was the chairman of the local Kennel Club and he entertained lavishly, holding banquets in a dining room you reached via a staircase lined with a collection of Gallé glass. First-time guests were teased by being asked to choose one of the numerous peppers served, each one hotter than the last. Meanwhile, outside in the garden he kept a pet crocodile, which later escaped and terrorised the local dogs.

KC's garden was beautiful, with centuries-old containers full of plants strewn over the garden, and he was also the chairman of the local Bonsai Society, the art of miniaturising trees that dates back to the Song Dynasty. As such he was the main judge of the Bonsai section of Hong Kong's annual flower show, organised by the Urban Council, and knowing of my interest in Chinese art and Tao aesthetics, he dragged me in as one of three judges, a position I continued in for five years. Westerners think Bonsai is a Japanese art form, partly because it is still practised there, but its origins are in the Song dynasty of China.

KC was also very adept at making money. He once told me that the US dollar would devalue within three months of the US pulling out of Vietnam as they had let down an ally, an opinion that went against the common thinking of the time which held that saving the sums spent on the war would make the dollar appreciate. He put his money where his mouth was and placed a big bet on gold. He also mentioned his opinion to the Canadian government who took his advice, and later on their recommendation he bought some real estate near Calgary.

Another of the great characters of Hong Kong was Sir RunRun Shaw, the movie mogul. He used to throw supper buffet parties for the movers and shakers of Hong Kong with around 100 guests a time and the supper would be followed by a showing of the latest Hollywood blockbuster in his private cinema. I would probably know about a fifth of the guests and we would be ushered in by starlets in gorgeous cheongsams, the traditional Chinese female dress.

RunRun's house was in the film company's complex in Clearwater Bay. Guests were dropped off at the entrance by their chauffeur, who would then take the car on to a car park, and be given a Chinese meal and watch some Kung Fu or porn movie. Ah Keung never seemed to mind the evening outings on these occasions, which occurred about twice a year.

A great loss came when my father Jack died on 4th April 1985, at the age of 80. He had been ill for some time as his heart began to fail. Nursed by Madge, he knew he was facing the end. He wrote us a letter looking back over his life, emphasising that in the difficult circumstances after my mother's death, he had done his best to provide Desmond and me with a decent education in order to set us up for life, but expressing some regret, too, that he had not been able to give us a family home when we were children. After his

COLLECTING CHINA

death, he was cremated and his ashes scattered in the sea near the flat in which he and Madge lived in Oak Bay, Victoria. It had been a very happy marriage and Madge was unsurprisingly depressed in the aftermath, so at my suggestion she travelled to the UK to visit her relatives, after which we arranged that I would drive her to Rannerdale, which she had heard about but never seen.

Her visit took place in June but we never made it to Rannerdale. We stopped at the Hilton Services just past Birmingham where Madge had a fall and broke her hip. An ambulance took her to Walsall General Hospital where by complete coincidence my old friend from Marlborough, Robin Fisher happened to be working. When I mentioned his name it emerged that he was the senior orthopaedic consultant surgeon at the hospital and indeed performed the operation (on the NHS, as he didn't practise privately), which was a success. Madge's family flew out from Canada while her sister in Cambridgeshire also arrived to look after her until her recovery was completed.

I continued to visit Madge about once a year when she was back in Canada until her death in 1993, when I represented the McElney family at her funeral in Victoria BC. When I was there I picked up one of the acorns from the Gary oak trees which are abundant in Oak Bay and planted it at Rannerdale, with a plaque nearby to say it was planted in Madge's memory. The last time I saw it, it was fifteen feet tall.

In 1988 I went on a long trip to South America, partly to celebrate the wedding of Christopher Johnson, my brother's stepson (his second wife Barbara's elder son), to a Brazilian girl, which took place in Itaul. I set off from Hong Kong and went via New Zealand, where I stayed at Wangerai with Neil Martin, Peggy's (née Davison) son. I had helped Neil through university in America; he obtained a first class honours degree in marine biology and is now based in Wellington looking after the Maori fishing rights.

From New Zealand I went on to Tahiti and Moorea where the movie South Pacific was filmed and where to my chagrin I found the lagoon was filthy. Because I had crossed the international dateline, I rolled up at the airport a day before my flight. From Moorea I went on to beautiful Bora Bora and from there to Easter Island, which was practically treeless, with nothing to recommend it other than the strange statues staring out to sea. From Easter Island I flew to Santiago, Chile, spending a couple of days there and flying on to Rio de Janeiro where a pickpocket tried unsuccessfully to get my wallet.

Rio has a most spectacular location, very similar to Hong Kong in many respects. From there I flew to Itaul and after about two hours flying I got off the plane but when my bags didn't appear I realised I'd got off at an intermediate stop. Fortunately the plane hadn't left and I was able to get back on and continue my journey. The wedding went well – I think Desmond and I were the only people in morning dress – with the reception at the bride's parent's ranch, which comprised acres and acres stretching into the distance. Chris is now a chartered accountant living in Sao Paolo.

After the wedding I went with Desmond, Barbara and Melinda, Desmond's step-daughter, to the Iguassu Falls, which are enormous, and on a par with Victoria Falls, and form the border between Argentina, Brazil and Paraguay. There is a perpetual rainbow at the Falls whenever the sun is out, and the hydroelectric power station supplies practically the whole of southern Brazil. After a brief trip to Paraguay, Desmond, Barbara and Melinda returned to Rio and the UK but I went on to Manaos on the Amazon, with its famous opera house, built in the rubber boom of the early 1900s. I spent a day in Brasilia en route, which is in the middle of nowhere but has a very impressive cathedral, wide avenues and other lovely buildings. Manaos is a thousand miles up the Amazon, on its junction with the Rio Negro, where I viewed the fresh water dolphins that inhabit the area.

I next went on to Lima, where I caught the train up to the Alto Plano and down the eastern side of the Andes, to Puno on Lake Titicaca where I took a boat to one of the floating islands. I then flew to Cuzco and saw the museum, and took the train to the station for Macchu Pichu, itself a memorable journey zig-zagging up the Andes foothills. From the station there was a bus ride up to the site itself which is truly spectacular and without which no tour of South America would be complete.

Another trip on my own was to Laos. I flew from Hong Kong to Luang Prabang, the capital and from there went to the extreme south of the country to view some Angkor-type temples before going north to the Plain of Jars, where I stayed in an auberge run by a Frenchman and walked onto the plain, a mile away. The enormous jars are all over the area and were probably for burial. The area figured prominently during the Vietnam War. Back in Luang, I took a boat on the crowded Mekong river to an impressive Buddhist shrine, stopping at very friendly villages along the way. I picked up a kidney-shaped basalt touchstone of a type found in the area in one village. Such touchstones were used in medieval times to test the purity or otherwise of gold, as they change colour when rubbed against a gold object depending on the purity of the gold.

A further excursion was to Bhutan for the Paro Festival where a huge thangka is unfurled before Paro's monastery, covering the whole façade. The flights in and out of Bhutan and the landing were not for the fainthearted, with rapid descents into a valley with soaring mountains, in a three-engined plane. Only 2,500 tourists per year were allowed into the kingdom at the time. I discovered that the ruler of Bhutan received tribute annually from

Assam and parts of Burma, with Asian rhino horn being part of that tribute. One djong (monastery) had a collection of such horns carved into Buddhist figures. Rhino horns were almost exclusively used to make cups, though there are a number of Wan-li marked pieces, in figure shapes. Other uses are recorded in literature, such as belt plaques, but have not been found.

Everywhere we went, magnolia, azalea, rhododendrons and poinsettia were blooming. The Bhutanese are expert archers and I sponsored a competition for the first to hit the bull with a US$100 as the prize. It was hotly contested for the sum was close to a man's monthly income at that time.

Although I was no longer engaged in the hands-on running of the firm, I continued to play a part in Hong Kong's legal profession throughout the 1980s. I was asked by the Hong Kong Bankers Association to look at the law of Property Ordinance that the government wanted to bring in, which I did with an articled clerk, Albert Chen, the best articled clerk I ever had, who later went on to become Dean of the Faculty of Law at the University of Hong Kong. We suggested about 150 amendments to the Ordinance: I was told that the government was so impressed by the quality of the work that they thought it had been done by a Chancery QC from London. In actual fact, it was Albert, under my supervision.

I was also a member of the Law Reform Commission for about five years, and chaired a sub-committee on the updating of the law of inheritance, intestacy and provision for wives and dependents who had been disinherited for some reason, which badly needed updating. It was a mishmash between the law as it was in England in 1843, as amended by local ordinances, and the fact that the Chinese had been told they could still have their customary laws of inheritance, as they stood in 1843, until they were amended by ordinances. Hong Kong had concubinage, so you could have as many wives as you wanted, and many different unusual marriage customs, up until 1971. These were all affecting the law of inheritance, with some very strange rules and regulations.

One problem was that under Chinese law, women were not allowed to inherit: they had maintenance until they got married and then a dowry on marriage. My sub-committee team and the government law draughtsman drafted three ordinances to bring the system in line with the modern world, with transitional provisions to deal with concubinage and other traditions.

We delivered the report in 1989 and there were problems: the Chinese in the New Territories didn't want women to get involved in the inheritance of the land and so held up the passing of the legislation until just before the takeover of Hong Kong by China. At that point the then-governor Chris Patten insisted that the laws be passed, not least because China doesn't disinherit women and so, some years after we had completed them, our recommendations were put into place without amendments. I was also Chairman of the Buildings Appeals Tribunal for about two years in the 1980s, after I had retired from the firm.

In February 1991 I flew to Mauritius for a three-day visit and gambled in one of the casinos, making £300, which I then blew on an undersea walk, complete with an enormous bell diving helmet, feeding the most beautiful array of tropical fish. This tourist attraction had been dreamt up by an Australian entrepreneur and Boris Becker had done the walk a few months beforehand. I hoped I might learn something from the entrepreneur about the whereabouts of a hitherto undiscovered shipwreck, and he didn't disappoint, telling me about a recovery from a wreck of a green piece, which from his description I thought was probably a thirteenth or fourteenth century Chinese celadon.

From Mauritius I went on to Nairobi and met up with Anne at the Aberdare Country Club. We were due to spend a week at Kitich Camp on the upper slopes of the Mathews Mountains, several hours' drive from Aberdare and famous for its collection of magnificent butterflies. Anne's driver took us to Wamba, where we were collected by a driver from the camp. While they were waiting for us, the camp cook and his assistant had been to the market to buy provisions but the driver was in such a hurry that he left without them.

In fact the driver was behaving in an increasingly peculiar manner, and we began to suspect he was drunk. We had nearly reached our destination just as evening was falling, when he managed to drive us into a ditch. We were effectively stranded, and in some danger from the lions which we could hear roaring nearby. Fortunately for us, our original driver, who had brought us from Aberdare, had noticed the abandoned staff and offered to take them in his own car to Kitich, and reached the site of our accident before any harm could befall us.

We didn't see many butterflies but had a rare sighting of a leopard, feeding on a goat carcass handily placed in a tree by the camp staff. Once he had eaten his fill, a genet sneaked up to take its turn. Our original driver stayed with us through the week at Kitich, and proved very knowledgeable about local birdlife, so I gave him my very expensive binoculars as a thank you for rescuing us. He then took us to join the Country Landowners' Association Tour of the Serengeti and Ngoro Ngoro crater, which was a very well-organised and enjoyable tour.

But there was more change in the air. By this time my collection, which was split between Hong Kong and Canada, had grown so large that I was beginning to turn my mind towards where it should be housed. I had at one stage planned to retire to Canada and as such had bought a flat in the Rudyard Kipling building in Oak Bay. However, as my father had now died, I decided to send the collection to the UK, and thought I would probably follow it.

And so, after more than thirty-five years working in the colony,

COLLECTING CHINA

a huge new chapter of my life was to start to open up. A museum was about to take shape.

CHAPTER 12
BEHIND THE SCENES AT THE MUSEUM

BY THE MID-1980s, I had nearly 2,000 pieces and there was a real concern about where it should all be kept. I had also by this time become involved in the more academic side of collecting: I had been made an Honorary Adviser on Oriental Art to the Hong Kong Museum of Art as well as other museums in Hong Kong and I had also written a number of articles on Chinese ceramics, jade and bamboo carvings, as well as giving lectures on the subject, so museums were very much on my mind.

To begin with, I had had no intention of setting up a stand-alone museum myself. It had never occurred to me to open a museum: rather, I thought that I would donate the collection to an institution that had already been established. I was maintaining a very open mind as to where that would be, but had decided that it would be best to house it in the UK. In 1986 on a trip to the UK, I began to investigate the options. My doctors had advised against spending much time in London on the grounds that it would be too stressful, but I had not entirely ruled it out and was making enquiries about whether an institution such as Asia House (New York) would be interested in establishing something similar in London. I was not the only person based in Hong Kong with a significant collection that was going to be housed elsewhere and it occurred to me that I might be able to set an example: if I brought my collection to the UK then other collectors might be encouraged to do likewise. I took the idea to the then-Minister of Culture, Sir Richard Luce, who was extremely dismissive of the plan, and so my collection ended up as one of only a few to come to the UK, the others going mainly to Canada or the United States.

By this time, though, I was certain that I wanted to find a permanent home for the collection in the UK. I got in touch with the Ashmolean Museum in Oxford and the Fitzwilliam in Cambridge, both of which were interested, but both of which made demands that made it impracticable for me to pursue it further. Lady Archer, a trustee of the Fitzwilliam, invited me to one of the colleges for lunch but then made it clear that if they were to take the collection, they also wanted a £5 million donation with which to construct a new building, which was totally unrealistic.

The Ashmolean initially seemed more positive and indeed my negotiations with them dragged on for eighteen months before hitting a brick wall. Initially they, too, asked for a donation, in this case £250,000 to build a new double-storeyed gallery, which I was happy to do. However, matters dragged on and on, the museum was closed two days a week at the time due to lack of resources and finally, in November 1989, negotiations came to an abrupt end. And so I began to feel that if my collection was going to end up in a museum, then perhaps it should be one that I founded myself, devoted mainly to my collection with additional pieces donated over time.

At this point several fortuitous circumstances came together. The first was that in 1988 the Rannerdale Trust that I had established acquired a building in Bath as an investment. Bath was chosen for a number of reasons: it is a civilised city with all the things I liked, including decent houses, decent restaurants and decent art galleries. It was also close to Desmond, who at the time was living in South Wales, cousin Anne in Buckinghamshire, and convenient for flights to Jersey, where I had set up the family trust. And it was also easy to get to the Lake District, where the family still owned Rannerdale Cottage.

And so in 1988 I contacted Betty Hollas, a friend I had met in Plymouth a decade previously and the only person I knew in Bath, and Betty asked her daughter Anne Challis to look for a property for me, initially as an investment but which might be suitable as a museum. She found the house at 12 Bennett Street which was up for auction. At that stage its future purpose was unclear and I was thinking of renting it out as flats, but when I acquired it, the ground floor and basement were occupied by a solicitor's offices, which meant that it did not have to be for residential use. While the Ashmolean talks were going on, we'd had an intimation that the building could be converted into a museum, so that provided a fall-back position which indeed was to prove very useful.

I got Betty and Robert Primrose to set up the museum as an educational charity and set the wheels in motion for the premises to become the Museum for East Asian Art. Betty and Robert then engaged the architect Michael Polkinghorne to convert the building and he also designed signage, lacquer furniture, the stationery and everything else, making a wonderful job of it all.

The legal work was done by Norton Rose, who submitted the planning application that allowed us to use the building, other than a flat on the top floor, as a museum. The Rannerdale Trust sold the building to the newly-formed charity for £220,000 (less than the price the Trust bought it for) and the ever-punctilious Betty rang the secretary of the head of the V&A's Oriental department to ask for advice on the best computer system to run the collection. The secretary at the V&A said she would ask her boss but forgot to close the line when she did so and so Betty quite clearly heard the reply: "Don't give them any help. They are our rivals."

COLLECTING CHINA

There was a certain amount of opposition in the early stages of applying for planning permission. Vivienne Rae Ellis, the then-chairman of the Circus Residents Committee – the Circus being Bath's famous curved terrace of Grade 1 listed townhouses dating from the Georgian era – spearheaded the concerns of the locals that the museum would house inferior objects, and their influence was brought to bear on the local councillors who had to approve the application. When I learned of these concerns I invited those residents, along with councillors and local museum personnel, to a dinner at the Royal Crescent Hotel, where I displayed about a dozen masterpieces that were to be housed in the museum to allay their fears. It did the trick: from then on, the residents of Bath were very positive about the museum. Vivienne Rae-Ellis in particular became a very active supporter and participant, serving on the management committee of the museum and providing invaluable assistance with early staffing matters. There was some friction, too, with Bristol Museum, which had its own Oriental collection, but that soon died down and it was accepted that Bath was now to have an Oriental museum of its own.

The fact that the museum was going to be based in Bath made up my own mind, and once planning permission for the museum came through – which took months – I too would buy a property in Bath, and spend part of the year there to oversee the set-up and early years of the museum, although had the collection gone to the Ashmolean I would probably have made Oxford my UK base. I again enlisted the services of Anne Challis, who showed me a few properties, finally coming up with Chapel House, 6a Sion Hill, which I liked on sight. I bought it and rented it out temporarily to Sir Christopher Curwen, a senior civil servant, before making it my own base when I was in the UK from May 1992. I arranged for all the pieces I had loaned to the Art Gallery of Greater Victoria to be shipped to Bath: in return and by way of thanks for what they had done, I gave them some duplicate Ordos bronzes and my entire collection of 20th century Chinese paintings.

There were about 350 artists represented in total, probably worth now about CA$10 million. I also gave them an eighteenth century rhino horn cup and a lovely bamboo lotus leaf brush washer. These gifts, incidentally, meant that I could effectively have lived in Canada tax free for the rest of my life as they would have counted against tax due annually. At that time there was no similar system in the UK for credit against tax when objects are given to a museum, except in the case of the donor's death, when the value of the object is excluded from the taxable estate, and therefore no benefit during one's lifetime, other than the kudos of giving the gift, which is a great shame. I understand a limited scheme is now in place.

By the time I came to spend some time in Bath, the museum was almost ready, with the showcases installed and preparations under way for the inaugural exhibition. It was an enormously busy time. Betty had organised a secretary and some staff, and meanwhile I was arranging for my furniture to be delivered, some from Hong Kong, where I was still resident most of the year, and some from Rannerdale. I was also taking delivery of the objects that were to be displayed in the museum, which were coming in from all over the world. There were pieces that had been in store in London and were shipped to Bath, a consignment from Victoria (which actually arrived after the opening) and some blue and white pieces which I had lent to the Hong Kong Club and were now making their way over here. And so, The Museum of East Asian Art in Bath, the first museum to be devoted solely to East Asian Art in the UK for thirty years, was born.

Nine months of frenetic work ensued in preparation for the inaugural exhibition which opened in April 1993: there was a great deal still to do. We published a two-part catalogue for the

COLLECTING CHINA

exhibition, which encompassed 225 Chinese ceramics, 90 pieces of Chinese metalware and over 40 pieces of Chinese decorative art, which included lacquer, bamboo carvings, softstone carvings and gourds dating from about 2500 BC to about 1820 AD. I had written the catalogues in Hong Kong before I came back, and most of the photography had also been done there, although some pictures had to be taken at the last minute and the photographer travelled from Hong Kong to complete the work.

The preface to the catalogue was written by the museum's first chairman, Roger Bluett, of whom more shortly, and we had a reception to mark the opening in the Assembly Rooms for about 200 guests coming from all over the UK and Hong Kong. John Julius Norwich performed the opening ceremony with a speech, followed by a lion dance with firecrackers performed by a team from Bristol. After the reception the guests went on to view the museum and were very impressed with what they saw. One of the guests was Sir Patrick Neill, who had won the Shell case for me, and who by now as Lord Neill was the Vice-Chancellor of Oxford and Warden of All Souls. He knew about the Ashmolean turning this opportunity down, and having seen the museum, his comment was that "Oxford's stupidity had been Bath's gain".

The first chairman, my old friend Roger Bluett, was the third generation of his family to deal in Oriental art in London. He had assisted me in the purchase of the tankard I had bought in 1968 but had had to sell on because I couldn't afford to keep it. Since then, I had bought quite a number of significant pieces from his shop in Davies Street near Bond Street station, including a white jade Dong Fang Shuo figure with peaches, a Xingyao black and white glazed bullock cart with passenger figure, a streaky-brown jade cup from the Newton Zoo sale and the nine dragon YungZhong underglaze red bowl.

Roger was very good to his clients and helped them build their collections, while at the same time his prices were not too high. And he was also extremely good to the museum. When he retired as chairman through ill health, he gave the museum the whole of the Bluett study collection that had been formed by the Bluett firm originally set up by Roger's grandfather in the 1920s, as well as the Sidney Smith study collection, of which he was trustee, as he thought the museum could make good use of it. The museum, it should be remembered, was registered as an educational charity, which remains one of its primary roles.

Roger also helped to establish the long-term financial health of the museum. We started the permanent endowment fund when he was chairman because at the time the trust which I had funded offshore when in Hong Kong was supporting the museum through donations of about £60,000 a year to pay the running expenses, and obviously subsidies on this scale were unsustainable and we resolved to start a permanent endowment fund.

I did, however, score a significant victory for all museums through a settlement with the tax office. I had received a letter from David Hartnett, then head of Her Majesty's Revenue and Customs (HMRC), confirming that donations from an offshore trust to the museum, which is an educational charity, were not taxable as long as the funds remitted were used for charitable purposes. The HMRC acknowledged this was a revised interpretation of a particular section and I thought I had achieved quite a victory for common sense in this matter.

Donations came in from many old friends as well as people who were simply interested in the field and were pleased that Bath now had the museum. Various small donations were raised by me during my visits to Hong Kong in the 1990s, and also came from anonymous donors. It was a process that went on for a very long time.

During the course of all this, my health continued to cause

problems and in 1997, during a period when I was in the UK, I realised when I was walking up a hill that I was suffering badly from shortness of breath. After consulting a doctor, I was informed I had angina and a triple heart bypass was recommended, which was made more risky by the fact that I had already had a stroke, with a two percent chance of me ending up in a vegetative state. A general anaesthetic could have caused terrible damage. So I took a second opinion from the eminent cardiologist Dr Robert Donaldson who was wary about the operation, telling me there was a fifteen percent chance of a vegetative state, and recommended instead an angioplasty, which meant inflating a balloon in the blocked artery to remove the blockage, a procedure that only needs a local anaesthetic and an overnight stay in hospital. The operation, done without a stent, was a great success.

The problem recurred in 2009 when I had a minor heart attack in Quito on the way back from the Galapagos and another angioplasty was done, this time with a stent, as they had improved markedly over the intervening twelve years. They had discovered that I had a 100 percent blockage in one artery, and an 85 percent blockage in another. The operation in Quito dealt with the first, but unfortunately I contracted a chest infection and I had to stay on for another ten days. I was accompanied home by a doctor and about a month later Dr Donaldson performed a third angioplasty, also with a stent, to clear the final blockage. The problem hasn't recurred since then.

A great deal of my time, however, was still devoted to fundraising. One of the people who left a major legacy to the museum in her will was an exotic creature called Johanna Joan Austin, who I had known since the very earliest days in Hong Kong. I originally met her through Marjorie Matheson, the manageress of the Helena May Institute. I used to play bridge with Marjorie and she introduced me to Johanna in the wake of a tragedy: the love of Johanna's life, a French diplomat, had just been killed in a car crash and years later she told me about their life together in Bangkok, where a python lived under the house and would slither out when they were entertaining guests. She was rather a racy woman and slightly shocked me at that first meeting, but we met up occasionally before she moved on elsewhere.

And that was that for nearly thirty years until she turned up again in Hong Kong in 1985 with an acquaintance of mine, a widower called Fred Hechtel, who owned an import/export company in the colony. He was a keen bird watcher and the two of them were off to watch Stellar's seal-eating eagles in Hokkaido. Johanna later told me that Fred had decided to re-qualify as a biologist; his subject was leeches and Johanna was used as their feeding ground. Johanna's interest in bird-watching never varied; she was a lifelong member of the Royal Society for the Protection of Birds and in later years, after we became friends, I saw her sitting still for hours at a time, watching birds such as a dipper make its dance.

And that, again, was that, until 1998 when she suddenly appeared in Bath, desperate for my help. She had fallen foul of the Inland Revenue, who had turned up at her flat in London and seized some of her property, claiming that she owed tax. I helped her by sifting through the evidence and deciding that through her late husband, she was domiciled in South Carolina and as such only liable to pay UK tax on income remitted to the UK. Johanna was living in a flat in Montagu Mansions that had been bought for her by a boyfriend for £15,000 in 1972. He had just left her £200,000 and I helped set her tax affairs in order, as well as becoming the executor of her will. When she was in Bath on that visit, we went to the museum, which she loved adding that she hoped to leave the value of her flat to the museum's endowment fund. At that point, I had no idea what she was really worth.

COLLECTING CHINA

Over the years we became good friends and on my visits to London to antique fairs, auctions and Oriental Ceramic Society lectures, of which she was also a member, I would take her to lunch or supper and she would keep me fascinated by telling me stories about her life. She was always pleading poverty and so I advanced her sums for anything from the upkeep of her flat to fixing her teeth, without ever realising that she had more money than I did. But she was lively and fun and I always enjoyed our time together.

Johanna Austin

Johanna's history came out in dribs and drabs. She was born in Lille to a German mother, the widow of a Dutch count, and had a half-brother living in Germany who inherited the title. Johanna's father was English and in the rag trade. Mother, son and daughter spent some time living in Germany before the war, and because her brother had by this time become a general in the Hitler Youth, they had to be smuggled out just before hostilities began, managing to make it to Yorkshire. Johanna was proud of her name, which she said was a Spanish aristocratic name passed down through her mother's side and her excellent German meant she occasionally taught it as an adult. She was educated at home and as a girl loved all animals, as she did throughout her life. She had a pet otter, which insisted on getting into the family's bath. After the war, she and her mother left her father and travelled across the continent, spending a lot of time in Italy and doing great walks, in one case from Milan to Rome. It was a habit she kept up in the 1950s, walking from Hanoi to Saigon in Vietnam.

BRIAN MCELNEY

A very adventurous woman, Johanna was in Morocco in 1961 taking photographs when a caravan of so-called "blue nomads" – actually Tuaregs, a tribe that lives in the Sahara – passed her and only she saw that a child had fallen off the back of the last lorry into the dust of the road. She hastened over, rescued the child and then took it on to the nomads' camp, where she was fêted as a hero, fed on sheep's eyes, which was a speciality kept only for honoured guests, and then, as a particular privilege, the chieftain asked if he could make her his fourth wife. Johanna declined, and made for the hills.

Johanna had taught skiing at St Anton in Austria when she was younger – she was notorious for her falls – and got to know a number of wealthy Europeans and Americans. In the late 1960s and 1970s this mutated into a service in which she accompanied rich Americans round the cities and art galleries of Europe, a service for which she was paid. She met her husband Talbot Patrick, a newspaper proprietor, in this way and he persuaded her to return with him to Rockhill, South Carolina, and when he fell terminally ill in 1977 he persuaded her to become his third wife, saying it would give her some financial security as his pension would provide for a widow; she mainly lived on this following his death in 1980. There were other men friends including a Portuguese count and a 'Name' at Lloyds, who bought her her flat.

However, her real love was for all things Chinese. Ever since she'd stayed in Hong Kong in the late 1950s and early 1960s she had been fascinated by Chinese art and culture and she returned to visit China in the 1980s. A few years later in 2008 when she happened to be in Hong Kong, I took her on a OCSHK trip to northwest China, the Gansu corridor, and Qinghai province, and so it was perhaps no surprise that she wanted to leave an endowment to the museum. She had wonderful taste, collected coins and became an expert on the coins of Indochina. She was a member of the Royal Academy until her death, as well as a member of the Royal Photographic Society, which she had joined as a teenager after producing award-winning photographs.

The last time I saw her was in 2013, when I took her for lunch at Wilton's in Jermyn Street for a birthday treat. Shortly afterwards she had a couple of heart attacks and was taken to hospital where, although they stabilised her condition, she died of pneumonia on 13th November 2013. I had wanted to see her, but I had fallen down a flight of stairs during a visit to my cousin Anne in October that year and damaged a vertebrae in the neck, leaving me with a permanent stoop and instructions to rest, so I was unable to visit. I was however, required to organise the death certificate, which involved a farcical journey around London, in the course of which I was directed variously around Westminster, Camden and the Harrow Road by a telephonist who turned out to be based in the north of Scotland – resulting in an angry letter to Westminster City Council. I also wrote and delivered the eulogy at her funeral.

After Johanna died, I saw her flat for the very first time and was a little shocked at how run down it had become. But nonetheless, Johanna died a wealthy woman. I collected piles of unopened letters, a haversack full of Chinese jades, snuff bottles and Tsuba, and a collection of coins which I put into a Waitrose bag and took to Baldwins, the coins auctioneer. They were put up for auction with an estimate of £90,000 – and actually sold for £353,000. There were no photographs in the flat and no address book, Johanna keeping much of her life story a mystery until the very end.

I knew that she had made me an executor of her will and I knew that she was leaving the value of her flat to the museum, but I did not know that she was leaving the rest of her estate as well until I received the will from Jersey. It was then quite a job tracking down her assets, which were scattered throughout the UK, Jersey, Hong Kong, and the US. I was at one point alerted to a deposit of

€160,000 when a receipt fell out of a book. And I was staggered when I learned how much she was really worth. The estate turned out to be almost £3 million, all of which went to the museum's permanent endowment fund.

CHAPTER 13
A Collector's Treasures

RUNNING A MUSEUM can be an expensive business and so apart from finding the right building, housing the collection and seeing to all the bureaucracy involved, it was important to establish a sound financial footing to secure the museum's future. When it first opened in 1993, the trust I had established agreed to pick up the cash flow deficit and I worked there on a voluntary basis from June 1992 to March 2010 helping to write catalogues and editing the object records prepared by the curator and marrying them with my own records. But it soon became obvious that a permanent endowment fund was needed to support the museum's running costs, as the amount brought in by the shop and the entrance fees was not going to be sufficient to cover these outgoings.

And so fundraising began and many people from my old life in Hong Kong were very helpful. The first £25,000 donation came from an old business associate, Jack Chia, followed by £100,000 from Madam Koo Yick Chan and her husband SL Wang. John Sheaff was another old acquaintance from the Hong Kong days: he was managing ICI when I acted on the sale of a warehouse property for the company involving P&O, which was unusual as we didn't often act for ICI. I heard from Brian Weedon, head of

BRIAN MCELNEY

John Sheaff

COLLECTING CHINA

GEC in Hong Kong, who had retired to Tetbury, near Bath, that John was interested in getting involved with the museum and we met up. John joined the management committee in about 1994. He started the record keeping of the PEF and together we acted as a management sub-committee to deal with investment for the PEF, appointing Brewin Dolphin as brokers and constantly badgered by Prim, who pointed out that it needed at least £2 million to be viable. John retired from the role in 2014.

Up until about 2007, I used to spend two or three weeks in Hong Kong every year fundraising for the PEF and was relatively successful. Along with the donors I have already mentioned, there was Albert, who was initially somewhat resistant to the idea but who eventually left us £150,000 in his will. Lucy Gomersall donated £25,000 and the Tyson family gave £50,000 in exchange for naming the scholar's studio, an area of the museum that recreates the environment in which a candidate for the office of mandarin would have studied, and as such contains not only furniture, but the wherewithal for painting, calligraphy and music.

The Primroses continued to be involved with the museum and also left a substantial donation in return for having a gallery named after them. Prim died in 2010 and Betty in 2012, at which point their bequest, of nearly half a million pounds, came into effect. These substantial amounts came to the museum after 2009 and until then the trust supplied about £60,000 a year to meet running costs, which was deemed to be tax free as it was being used for charitable purposes. Another of my trusts with assets of slightly over £1 million, was vested in the museum in 2008, with its collection, which had been on loan to the museum anyway, becoming a permanent part of the collection.

By 2008, the income from the permanent endowment fund which resulted from these donations, together with other income from entrance fees, shop sales and so on, for the first time removed the need for further subsidies, securing the museum's financial future once and for all.

In 1995, Roger Bluett stepped down as chairman and was succeeded by Air Chief Marshall Sir Michael Armitage, who I met as we were both members of the Bath and County Club and who had served in Hong Kong for three years. "I wrote to HRH Prince Michael of Kent, who is keen on China, to become a patron," Sir Michael recalls and the Prince opened our Japanese exhibition in 2002. It was also Sir Michael who recommended me for a high national award. The Honours Committee decided this should be an OBE, which I received in 2003 for my work on the museum.

Alan White, a retired ambassador to Chile who lived in Bath, became our next chairman and headed the museum for five years. He was succeeded by Ian Hay Davison, also now living in Bath. Ian had been the head of global accountants Arthur Anderson and was the executive chairman of the insurance giant Lloyd's of London during the period it was reeling under the scandal caused by asbestos and other huge insurance claims which were subsequently found to have been foisted on to Lloyd's "names." It was the most turbulent time in that institution's history and Ian did a great deal of work in sorting out unscrupulous dealings and setting the insurance market right. He subsequently did further sterling work merging three Hong Kong stock exchanges, which is when I met him. He was responsible for cleaning up murky business dealings, sacking the chairman of the Far East Exchange who subsequently went to jail for taking bribes, and imposing new regulations which helped to curb buccaneering business practices in the market. He was a highly effective chairman, greatly shortening the length of our museum committee meetings.

Our first female chairman was Anne Shepherd, who took on the role in 2014. She had been the executive secretary to Chris Patten, now Lord Patten, the last governor of Hong Kong. She was

COLLECTING CHINA

thus steeped in civil service practice and also brought a greater efficiency to running the meetings and streamlining the reports coming into the management committee.

The museum's logo is an Ordos bronze dating from about 600BC and it came into my possession in circumstances briefly mentioned in Chapter 10 but which merit a longer account here as it was part of a collection of bronzes that are now in the possession of the museum. They were part of the F.A. Nixon collection, Nixon being an Englishman resident in China since the 1920s, teaching English at Tientsin university. He moved to Hong Kong after the war, inhabited a room in the Hong Kong Club and died in 1974 at the age of 96. Some years before he died, he sold his collection of Nestorian crosses to the Fung Ping Shan museum, now the Hong Kong University Museum, which bought it with the help of funds from the Lee Hysan family. This was the largest collection of such crosses in the world: they are not all cross-shaped and they are probably artefacts of the Ongut Mongols, who were mainly Nestorian Christians who occupied part of the Eurasian steppe

Anne, Betty Primrose and Prim at my OBE celebrations (2003)

200

from the tenth to the thirteenth century. No two examples are the same and they were probably the nomads' personal seals.

In 1994, the year after the museum opened, we mounted an exhibition entitled "Jades from China." *The Independent* called it "the most important exhibition of Chinese jades to be put on anywhere in Europe for more than twenty years," and it featured 350 carvings from China's Neolithic period, around 5500BC to about 1800AD. It had a 400-page catalogue complete with 430 illustrations, which I had spent a year writing, with help from previous catalogues written by James Watt and Barry Till, which included many of my jades and were a mine of relevant information. Angus Forsyth also contributed chapters on Neolithic jades.

My relationship with the Art Gallery of Greater Victoria had remained a strong one. Barry Till, had taken over from Colin Graham in running the Oriental collection of the museum, and arranged many exhibitions using my pieces, some of the most significant being porcelain of the High Qing and jades from China.

I took two trips led by Barry Till. The first of these in 1994 was a truly memorable six-week trip to Tibet, Vietnam and Cambodia with my step-sister Magsie Oliphant as one of the fellow travellers and in the first of these countries we saw Lhasa, the Potala and Seceral monasteries, Gyantse and the Sakya Monastery with its library of centuries-old Buddhist texts. The monastery is of such importance that it is the Buddhist equivalent of St. Catherine's monastery in Sinai to Christians; the upper library had been totally destroyed by the Red Guards despite the fact that the State Council had previously declared it a protected monument, an act of terrible cultural vandalism.

Barry spoke Chinese and had met the Dalai Lama: he carried a picture of him on the journey and so was greeted warmly by the locals everywhere. The journey was not without its hair-raising moments: in the bus crossing the passes we got up to 20,000 feet and we were also ferried across the Tsangpo river which later becomes the Brahmaputra when it enters India. From the crossing point we drove in a truck a short distance to Samye monastery, which had wonderful paintings on its walls of the Buddhist paradise dating back to the Tang dynasty. We witnessed a ceremony there for the dead with enormous trumpets wailing and met a leather-masked beggar, the masking being what all beggars were expected to do. Ever on the look-out for collectables, I bought an attractive silver sheathed knife from one of our fellow passengers on the ferry.

From there we travelled to Vietnam, to Hanoi and the Ho Chi Minh Museum where I came across mention of his time with the (incorrectly-named) Lawyer Lose, actually Loseby, described in the second chapter of this book – I wrote to them pointing out their error. From Hanoi we travelled to Hue and Danang, where we visited the museum with its Champa artefacts and took a trip on the Perfume River, before going on to Ho Chi Minh city, formerly Saigon and still known to many inhabitants as such. We visited the museum there as well as taking a short trip outside to the Cu Chi tunnels, the extraordinary underground network used by the Vietcong when they were fighting the Americans. It is possible to crawl through some bits but I chose not to, but it did illustrate why the Americans didn't stand a chance in that conflict.

While in Ho Chi Minh City, I bought an Annamese brownish-green glazed bowl decorated with incised boys in a style copying Chinese Qingbai bowls of early 13th century, to which period I believed this bowl also belonged, which was then confiscated by the customs at Ho Chi Minh airport. I suspect this was a carefully prepared scam: no doubt the guide who had taken us to the antique market had tipped off the customs and the piece duly went back for resale to the next tourist to be fleeced.

From there, it was on to Cambodia and its capital Pnomh Penh, where we saw the Killing Fields with its stupa of skulls and then on to Siem Reap and the magnificent sites of Angkor Wat and Angkor Thom.

Another trip which combined travel with collecting was a visit to Tibet in 2003, in pursuit of knowledge about an unusual object I acquired in Hong Kong in the mid-1980s. It was a small, rectangular four-legged incense burner which was quite unlike anything I had seen before, and after consulting a very experienced dealer I was told it was an example of Tibetan "Derge" work dating from about 1425-1435. Derge is a principality on the border of Tibet and Sichuan Province and is now a part of Sichuan Province although when the work was produced it would have been in Eastern Tibet. I was to buy more Derge pieces over the years, all of which are now in the museum. The best pieces were produced by Horbo metalworkers, an area within Derge, about whom not a great deal was known.

I resolved to visit to find out for myself what I could, and so in 2003 set off with a driver and an interpreter in a four-wheel drive to make the three-and-a-half-day journey from Chengdu to the small village of Horbo. The drive there, which encompassed several mountain ranges, was spectacular. We drove at well over 12,000 feet for much of the way, stopping in the town of Ganzi, where we dined on yak stew. Indeed, yaks were much in evidence, grazing in the fields as we made our 1,900 kilometer journey, finally arriving in the village and valley of Horbo, close to the upper reaches of the Yangtze River. I was able to quiz a senior metalworker, Mr Trolo, who had been sent questions in advance, visit his workshop and place of business, before being presented with a selection of three knives to choose from. I bought one for about £16 and was told that I had chosen the best of the lot. There was then the three-and-a-half-day drive back again, in the course of which we stopped again in Ganzi for lunch and met a reincarnated monk.

Most of the hotels we stayed in on this trip had the usual

COLLECTING CHINA

Chinese-style (drop) toilets but in one we found a Western-style toilet. However, we discovered it had not yet been connected, so effectively worked in the same way as the others. To this day, I'm not sure whether it was there only for effect or whether they simply hadn't got round to connecting it.

The second trip with Barry was in 2004 to Outer Mongolia, where we visited sites where dinosaur eggs had been discovered, saw the Naadam festival at Ulan Bator and flew by helicopter to Karakorum, the Mongolian capital of Genghis Khan's son and successor, Ogedei Khan, which was totally destroyed by a Ming Chinese army led by General Xu Da in 1388. It now consists of just a Buddhist monastery called Erdene Zuu, surrounded by a low wall, surmounted with a series of stupas. Nearby is a stone tortoise, which once held a stele with a Mongolian imperial decree.

In August 2006, I spoke at a conference on Portuguese shipwrecks held at Moussel Bay in South Africa's Cape Province. I had recently completed my catalogue of Chinese ceramics and the maritime trade pre-1700, which had taken me two years to research and write, involving a great deal of work and several trips, including to Fuzhou, the capital of Fujian province, the Philippines and Sri Lanka, which was an important destination for ceramics, with numerous finds from the Tang dynasty onward. A lot of the information in that volume is difficult, if not impossible, to find elsewhere. From this catalogue, I had written a paper on trade in Chinese ceramics and imperial decrees affecting ceramic exports, and it was this I was to present at the conference.

The conference was organised by Valerie Esterhuizen, and alongside the conference sessions she had arranged a tour of Portuguese wreck sites along the South African coast, which enabled me to confirm much of my research as the dates of all the wrecks were known and ranged from 1552 through to about 1624. The fabulous bonus of this trip was the sight of whales and their

At Buckingham Palace to receive my OBE (2003)

calves playing in the waves of the bay.

During the trip to Sri Lanka, I stayed in a lovely hotel at Dumballa where a monkey came into my room when I was out to steal the tea and sugar. It shot off on my return.

The museum had lots of maritime ceramics (i.e. specifically designed for export), which we decided to exhibit, hence the catalogue, and we were lucky enough to find a sponsor in Li & Fung, one of Hong Kong's biggest trading companies and still controlled by a Hong Kong Chinese family. The exhibition was to form part of their 100th anniversary celebrations, and after being shown in the museum in 2007, it moved to Hong Kong in 2008.

Travel and Chinese art remained two of the most important facets of my life but there was more, as well. My long-standing interest in history prompted me to think about a novel, and I was also to experience the death of yet another close friend.

Old China Hand

ALTHOUGH THE MUSEUM has been the focus of much of my energy and attention over the last twenty-five years, there have been other projects, too. I have been an avid reader all my life, of history, Chinese art and also of historical novels, another artistic pursuit encouraged by my old schoolmaster Audemars as well as his fellow teacher, Mr Shaw. The latter taught Latin and Greek history and one period we studied in detail was the decline of the Roman Empire from 120BC to the Battle of Actium in 31BC.

These various interests came together around the year 2000 when I read with great curiosity a five-volume abridgement of Joseph Needham's masterpiece *The History of Science and Civilisation in China*, from which I developed a lecture on the primacy of Chinese inventions, analysing why, having been so far ahead in scientific knowledge, China allowed the West to catch up and eventually overtake them. For example, in 2008 or 2009, while visiting Buddhist sites in Gansu and Qinghai province with Johanna, we came across the site of a neolithic Palace dating from before 2000BC, which had a concrete floor! Apparently the gravel, sand and lime used to make concrete today were available locally and were used widely in that province but their use did not spread beyond that province to the rest of China. Traditionally the Romans are credited with the invention of concrete.

Within Joseph Needham's text there was a passage detailing the battle of Xiungnu in 36BC, after which 145 soldiers were captured. It was thought that they were Roman because they had been seen practising testudo, a kind of military formation that was used solely by the Romans, which involved moving in a tortoise formation and using their shields to cover themselves completely. I thought that they must have come from among the 10,000 captives taken to Magiana by the Parthians after the battle of Carrhae and realised there was potential here for an interesting historical novel.

I started to research the story of Carrhae and the Chinese sources about the battle in which the 145 Romans were captured. There was quite a lot of information about the episode and I was quickly able to sketch out a plot. However, there was a problem about writing it myself. I was heavily involved with the museum and writing up my knowledge of Chinese art, so I decided to employ a ghost writer.

I was put in touch with Andrew Primrose (no relation to Betty and Robert) by a friend called Keith Painter, chairman of Bristol's British Commonwealth Society and a member of the Bath & County Club. Andrew, the son of the then Vicar of Thornbury, had just finished a degree in English Literature and I gave him my research covering both the Chinese and Roman sides of the story. Over the next year or so he wrote it up and sent me each chapter as he finished it. I returned it with corrections and suggestions. Andrew lived during some of the time he was writing in Sri Lanka and Hong Kong and actually went to the town in the Gansu corridor where the Romans had been settled, following the track of the novel's hero. He also travelled along the probable route they had trodden to get the ambience of the area, though the area is a lot drier today.

In 2002 I celebrated my 70th birthday which is a particularly auspicious birthday to the Chinese and the day on which the emperor used to present his senior mandarins with a cane with a handle adorned according to their position – a bird if the mandarin was a civil official, or a lion or other animal if a military mandarin.

Andrew Primrose visiting Li-qian, the town in the novel

The handles could be ivory or jade and could vary to reflect the rank of the mandarin concerned – I have in my collection an ivory handle with lion.

There was party in Bath to celebrate the occasion and there was a big turnout, some people coming from Hong Kong. Among the invitees was Madam Koo Yick Chan (also known as Mrs S.L. Wang), who had been a very demanding client of mine, wont to station a staff member outside my office waiting for me to produce an important agreement. It was she who came to the hospital with bowls of expensive sharks fin soup to speed my recovery after my stroke and was a significant donor to the museum's PEF. She was not able to come to my 70th party but sent me a cheque as a birthday present. I used this to pay for a tour of Central Asia, visiting some of the places that must have figured in the Roman story, such as the ruins of Nisa, 18 kilometres south west of Ashgabat, the capital of Turkmenistan.

And so, again, I was able to combine my love of travel with another of my interests. I flew first to Kazakhstan and then drove to Kyrgyzstan to the far end of Lake Issul Kul, visiting and camping in a mini grand canyon where some German geologists were studying. In the course of our conversation it emerged that they did not believe me when I said the Chinese knew fossils were extinct animals one thousand years ago; I sent them the reference in Needham. I then drove up the Torugut pass, over which the Chinese must have taken their prisoners and saw a caravanserai on the way. I then proceeded to Dzanbul which is close to the area where the ephemeral capital of the Xiungnu leader would have been.

During our drive in Kyrgyzstan the driver was caught speeding through a village and fined on the spot – $5 with receipt or $1 without. Half way through the trip, I joined a tour with a party of others organised by Steppes East and visited Tashkent, Samarkand

and Khiva, and the Ferghana valley touching Afghanistan, Uzbekistan, and other of the "stan" countries in the region. The old buildings in Tashkent and Samarkand were disappointing, being mostly extensively repaired or entirely rebuilt in contrast to the splendours of Isfahan where the originals are still intact. I eventually flew out from Biskek to Thailand and Hong Kong.

The novel was finished by 2004 and I submitted a synopsis to several literary agents but there was no follow up and I got a little tired of the project. It would make a splendid film.

Andrew Primrose helped me on another project, too, albeit a sadder one. On October 27th 2009, after a year of ill health, my old friend Albert Sanguinetti died in Hong Kong. Glowing tributes were paid to him across the board, among them by Mr Justice Kemal Bokhary, vice-president of Hong Kong's Final Court of Appeal. It subsequently emerged that Albert had requested that a biography be written of his life and I undertook this task, as he had requested I do, about a decade previously. Until then, my own ill health had prevented me from taking on the task but I spent time in Hong Kong speaking to his friends and acquaintances, and presented his family with a first draft. To date they have not yet decided how they want to proceed with this project.

Much of the last two decades had been taken up with the museum and frequent trips back and forward between my home in Hong Kong and the museum's base in Bath. In 2011, I finally decided to relocate to Bath permanently and now live not too far from my cousin Anne and other family members.

Desmond now divides his time between Portugal and the UK. He had three children with his first wife, Wilma, who died in 1980. My niece, Susan Ariel was born in 1963 and trained as a lawyer at UCL, doing a stint at JSM in the summer after her first year and co-hosting a party with me where she was fascinated to meet the Chinese entrepreneurs and business people I dealt with on a daily

COLLECTING CHINA

basis. She now has two sons, Cameron and Tristan.

My two nephews are Gerald Andrew, born in 1965 and now resident in the Philippines with his wife and family, and Mark Douglas Shane, who was born in 1966 and also spent some time with me in Hong Kong in the early 1980s. He went on to build an extremely successful foreign exchange business which he eventually sold to the Bank of Ireland. He has a daughter called Molly.

Desmond's second wife Barbara died in late 2009 after taking Desmond and I to Ecuador and the Galapagos. She had been diagnosed with a malignant brain tumour and stated that she didn't want to give the Chancellor money so she would spend it on this trip. We went in May 2009 and it was at the end of this trip that I had the heart attack in Quito.

Madge, Desmond, Jack and Wilma with (behind) Susie, Mark, and Gerry (Fawnridge 1980)

BRIAN MCELNEY

With Desmond in Ecuador, en route to the Galapagos

My eyesight has been failing since 2011, and as a result my travel activities have been confined to gentle river cruises and short visits to European cities.

In recent years I have been given various honours: I was accorded an honorary MA by the University of Bath in 1997 in recognition of my contribution to education in establishing the museum as an educational charity, and was made an OBE in 2003 in recognition of my contribution to the museum of both my collection and my expertise. I have remained actively involved with the museum, lecturing, writing for its journals and showing visitors around, as well as continuing to raise funds for its permanent endowment fund.

Now settled into an apartment overlooking Bath's famous Abbey, I can ponder a lifetime in a world that has changed beyond all recognition since my childhood, and for the purposes of this book have amused myself by compiling a list of twenty-five objects which have been significant in my life.

When I started collecting Oriental art, the popular conception was that it was exotic, generally over-decorated and difficult to understand, with much of it poor quality. This view was understandable as most examples seen by the man in the street were 19th and early 20th century specimens of Chinese porcelain made for the mass export market when China was in serious decline.

My collection has been a lifetime's work of concentrated effort to seek out the best, and I hope it can put to bed this misconception and demonstrate that China has produced some of the most exquisite art in the world.

I think I always intended that my collection would end up in a museum and from the early 1970s this had some influence on my collecting habits. I found myself instinctively filling in the gaps in the collection to cover as broad a spectrum as possible with the best examples available.

You are only a custodian of the objects you collect, and when it is a significant collection one has a duty to ensure its survival, which is what I hope I have done by putting it on public display and ensuring the stability of the funding to maintain it.

It has given me great pleasure, and is a source of great pride.

My Life in Twenty-Five Objects

In 2010 the British Museum and Radio 4 combined forces to produce a monumental project, compiled and presented by the then British Museum Director Neil MacGregor and ultimately the subject of a book, "A History of the World in 100 Objects", which purported to be a history of humanity illustrated through pivotal objects that each represented in some way human development through artistic and scientific progress. The project was a deserved and resounding success and the idea was such a good one that it has been adapted to numerous differing endeavours, including the last chapter of this book.

I have spent my life collecting objects. It has been, in addition to my practice as a solicitor, in many ways my life's work. But almost all of us to a degree collect objects in some respects and while we might not be defined by our possessions, at the same time they can define our own personal histories. A painting, a statuette, a very familiar household item, can act as the Madeleine in Proust's *A la Recherche du Temps Perdu*, bringing to mind a person, a story, an event. And in my case they also chart the growing fascination I found in art generally and more specifically in the Chinese and Oriental art that is now on display in the museum. And so this is the history of my life – in twenty-five objects.

	**Napoleon mirror with eagle and ball.** I've known it all my life. It originally belonged to one of my great great great grandfathers – William Ransford (1780-1844) or Thomas Gay Ransford (1788-1851) – and I grew up with it in first Liverpool and then Rannerdale. It brings back an England now lost in the mists of time.
	**Coronation goblet.** This was my first purchase as a collector, bought from Heal's Tottenham Court Road for £9 in 1953, when I was living in London and doing my Articles. It has a beautiful red, white and blue spiralling filament in the stem and is another mark of a moment in history, in this case the coronation of Britain's longest serving monarch.
	**Sino-Tibetan gilt brass Buddha with unopened base.** Dating from the 17th century, this was my first Oriental art purchase, acquired in 1955 in a small antique shop in the passageway between Brompton Road and Earl's Court station, near where I lived, for £26, more than half a month's allowance back then. The V&A wrongly ascribed it to the 19th century but translated the inscription as a blessing. It is unusual to have an unopened base which means it can still be prayed to and was the first proper indication that I was to spend my life collecting Oriental art.
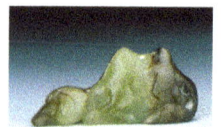	**Jade Bactrian camel.** Probably intended for use as a brush rest. This was an early jade purchase for less than £5 in about 1970 that has now been dated and accepted as Tang or Sui dynasty. The piece confirmed my eye in regard to jade and I have since written and lectured on the subject. James Watt was in the forefront of establishing a chronology for post-Han jades at the time of my purchase and this piece helped him in his endeavours.

	**Blue and white early Kangxi beaker delicately painted with a bird on a branch.** It has a Chenghua mark but is actually early Kangxi c1662-1677. This is my favourite period for ceramics as many mandarins who had lost their jobs with the change in dynasty in 1644 from Ming to Qing turned their hand to decorating porcelain, and the delicacy of the painting at this time is striking. This is a good example and it was an early acquisition from Tai Sing for probably too low a price (HK$700).
	**Blue and white transitional fish bowl.** c1640, purchased in a Bangkok curio shop full of fakes for US$200. Although it was covered with dirt when I purchased it, I noticed the tell-tale V-tick grasses typical of the transitional period from 1625 to 1675. I took it into the bath with me and all the mud and dirt fell off and revealed the piece in all its glory.
	**Bamboo carving of three frogs.** Dated 1623, bought for HK$2,500. This was the first bamboo piece I was ever offered, and as it is dated precisely to the year, it is arguably the most important bamboo carving known, as other bamboo only have cyclical dates and there is uncertainty about which sixty-year cycle is applicable. It is known that the artist who carved it was the student of a third generation member of the Zhu family of bamboo carvers, so this piece takes the dating of carving bamboo as an art form back to at the least the mid-16th century. I became a serious collector of bamboo carvings after this purchase, bringing the finest to Bath and giving one to Canada and about twenty to the Hong Kong Museum of Art.

COLLECTING CHINA

	**Blue and white foliated dragon bowl with square lip protrusion.** Acquired in Macassar (now Ujung Pradang) in 1972. I wrote about dating of foliated dragons in the Hong Kong Oriental Ceramic Society Bulletin, placing this at c1510 but have since revised the dating (as listed in the Museum's journal) to the 1450s.
	**White nephrite jade bowl.** I purchased this from Brian Spark's widow. This exquisite bowl was given to Brian by his brother John Spark as a wedding present. Jade of this quality became available in 1740 when the Emperor commissioned 100 pieces to be carved. A similar bowl with provenance to John Spark sold for many tens of thousands of pounds c2009.
	**Fat-tailed sheep in nephrite jade of lychee-flesh colour.** Fat-tailed sheep are known to have arrived in China in the early 11th century from central Asia; I saw one in Uzbekistan in 2003. The colour of the stone, christened lychee-flesh, started to come into China in 951 and continued to arrive until 1028; thereafter jade of this precise colour is very rare. I purchased it for AU$750 in the Southern Cross Hotel, Melbourne in 1974.
	**Small yellow and green Yingzhong mark and period wine cup.** This colour combination is reserved for the first or second rank of concubine. Its small size makes it a rare survival. When I saw it first it had been reserved for T.Y. Chow, a major collector in Hong Kong and I thought I had missed it. A few days later I met T.Y. Chow at the races and he told me he had decided not to buy the piece as it was too small and insignificant. I went straight to Tai Sing's shop from the race course and bought it for HK$7,000.

	**Yongzhong *famille rose* brush pot with simulated bamboo frames and *faux bois* corner panels.** This unmarked piece was described by the Hong Kong art dealer and collector Eddie Chow as one of the finest brush pots he had ever seen. The *faux bois* (fake wood) panels was an innovation of this period and the date (1723-1735) is confirmed by the inclusion of purplish pink on one of the floral panels, a colour that dates to pre-1729 by which time the pink of the *famille rose* palette had been perfected.
	**Carved red lacquer saucer.** With Imperial dragon and Wanli Imperial six character mark written down the centre of the base in the style of the Jiajing reign's marks, it is therefore dateable to 1572 or 1573. The piece is significant as there were numerous old repairs and the fifth claw of the Imperial dragon had been carefully carved away to disguise its Imperial origin. I found it in 1976 when Aunty Mary and I were touring Italy; at the time it was in a dreadful condition as it was being used as an ash tray in an antique shop in Florence. I bought it for about £30.
	**Yixing teapot by Yang Pengnian with calligraphy by Chen Mansheng.** This piece was shown in Hong Kong in 1980, when the potters from Yixing all agreed the calligraphy was that of the famous mandarin who revived the kiln in the early 1800s. Four other pieces purportedly also inscribed by him were in the same show but this was the only one they agreed had his genuine writing.

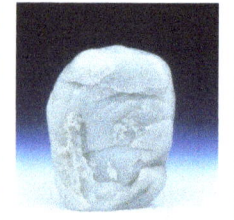	**Carved celadon-coloured jade mountain with Qienlong Imperial inscription dated 1774.** I found this in the King's Road in Chelsea in the mid-1970s, where it was being sold as a carved green stone mountain for £300. I was surprised that the London dealer did not know the piece was jade, given its date.
	**Lead Bactrian camel.** From a Tang shrine c700AD, which I acquired on the Dunhuang trip in 1982. This piece has a plug at the bottom and would have fitted into a lead altar triptych with a Buddha and two bodhisattva (those on the journey), as one of the animals on the plinth of the altar.
	**Ming ivory cane handle with Asian lion finial with a Chinese inscription.** Acquired for HK$3,600. The Emperor used to give canes to his senior mandarins when they reached the age of 70; a cane surmounted with an animal if a military mandarin or bird if a civil mandarin, appropriate to their rank. I have seen several with bird finials but this is the only example of a military cane handle I have seen and it is a great rarity. There are worn but still visible characters on the underside, which is probably the name of the recipient.
	**Qingbai melon-shaped ewer with long spout.** Acquired in Macau with K.Y. Ng in 1983, the one and only time I went to Macau specifically to see something special. Up to that point, since Deng Xiaoping took over in 1978, a lot of pieces came to Hong Kong from mainland China via Macau, but in 1983 this flood became a trickle and the piece is significant as marking the end of the golden years for collectors. An identical piece was excavated from a tomb dated 1099, so this can be dated firmly to the 11th century.

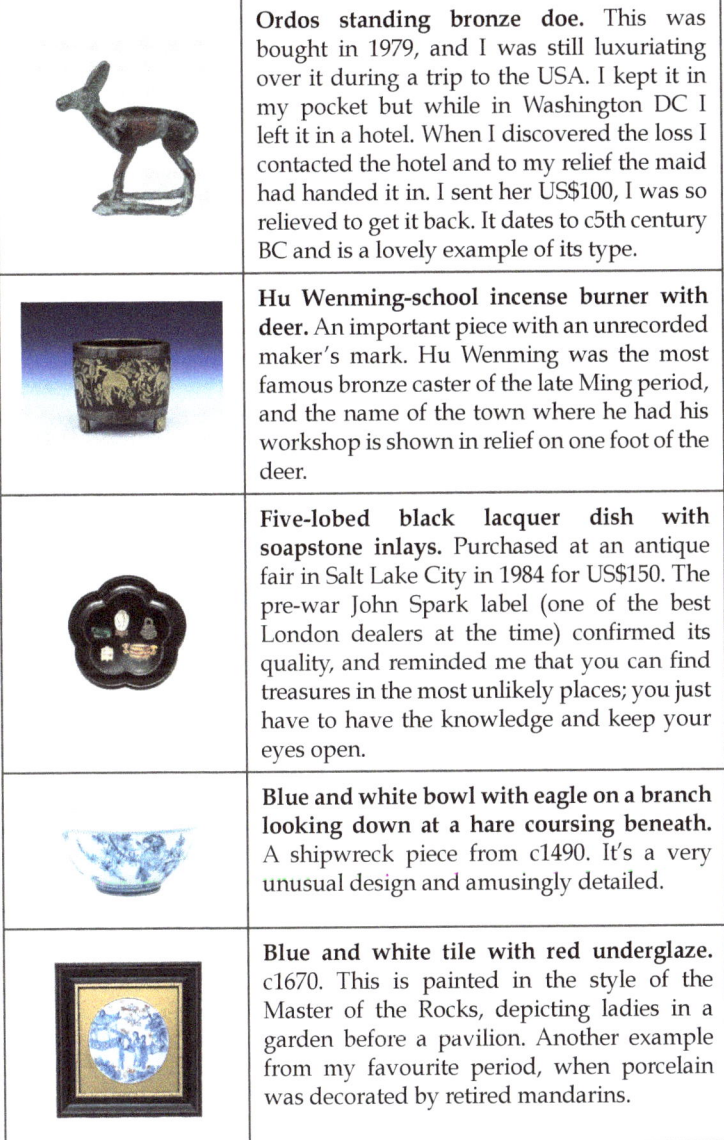

Ordos standing bronze doe. This was bought in 1979, and I was still luxuriating over it during a trip to the USA. I kept it in my pocket but while in Washington DC I left it in a hotel. When I discovered the loss I contacted the hotel and to my relief the maid had handed it in. I sent her US$100, I was so relieved to get it back. It dates to c5th century BC and is a lovely example of its type.

Hu Wenming-school incense burner with deer. An important piece with an unrecorded maker's mark. Hu Wenming was the most famous bronze caster of the late Ming period, and the name of the town where he had his workshop is shown in relief on one foot of the deer.

Five-lobed black lacquer dish with soapstone inlays. Purchased at an antique fair in Salt Lake City in 1984 for US$150. The pre-war John Spark label (one of the best London dealers at the time) confirmed its quality, and reminded me that you can find treasures in the most unlikely places; you just have to have the knowledge and keep your eyes open.

Blue and white bowl with eagle on a branch looking down at a hare coursing beneath. A shipwreck piece from c1490. It's a very unusual design and amusingly detailed.

Blue and white tile with red underglaze. c1670. This is painted in the style of the Master of the Rocks, depicting ladies in a garden before a pavilion. Another example from my favourite period, when porcelain was decorated by retired mandarins.

COLLECTING CHINA

	**Painting of Saanich farms.** By Colin Graham RCA (1915-2010), curator at the Art Gallery of Greater Victoria. Colin presented this to me after my donation of 350 Chinese 20th century paintings to the art gallery; it is inspired by one of the paintings I donated, by Huang Bin Hung (1865-1955).
	**George III silver tea caddy.** Sold at auction in Hong Kong in the late 1960s as an 'oval tin box'. Albert and I both knew it was more than that - not least because it was clearly silver marked for 1785. He left a bid of HK$70 with the auctioneer but didn't attend the auction; I did attend, and warned him that if it went over HK$70 I would bid for it. Albert left it to me in his will.

Acknowledgements

THE WRITING OF THIS biography would not have been possible without the help of Virginia Blackburn, whose skills as a biography writer are well attested. She has managed to assemble and render my memories, stretching over eight decades, into a chronological and coherent whole.

Inevitably as I recorded these memories, they stimulated further anecdotes and her readiness to revise the text to include such extras was gratifying.

My thanks also go to my secretary Julie Ticehurst who worked tirelessly on my memoirs and the chapters as they arrived for review.

I also wish to thank Colin Sheaf for writing a fulsome foreword to the biography and for his helpful comments on the changes which affected the London market for Chinese art in the late sixties; and Sir Michael Armitage, Isabel Ponting and Dominic Regan for reading the final manuscript.

And to Neil Watson for the beautiful photographs of some of my collection, and for digitalising old family photographs for publication.

Thanks are also due to my old friends and colleagues from Hong Kong and the Museum of East Asian Art, and of course my family, who have supported and encouraged me in this endeavour.

Fortunately my memory for what interested me - namely art, history and the extraordinary development of Hong Kong – proved reliable and we have produced a biography which includes descriptions of my numerous trips over the years, tells the story of my collection, and the development of Hong Kong from its pre-war status of a relative backwater to its blossoming into the third most important financial centre in the world.

Brian McElney
Bath, March 2017

Jack's Letter

Friday March 9th 1984
To the Family

I've long since forgotten what medical knowledge I did have but at least I can assess some of the basics and I realise that the signs of heart failure first apparent about 2½ years ago are now increasing rapidly.

First of all 'shortness of breath' on any physical effort and then, since that undesignated illness in mid- and late January, oedema of ankles and feet which has become progressively worse despite treatment by cardiologists, etc.

So I feel that the time has come when I must face up to the inevitable and just hope that in my remaining weeks or months I can give as little trouble as possible to my family, especially Madge, who has been wonderful and despite her own frailty has laboured so assiduously on my behalf.

I've had a good innings and can't grouse. There are some things I'd like to have done differently but in the main I'm satisfied.

I trust all will go well with you all.

Jack

COLLECTING CHINA

Victoria 9th May

My dear Family (I include Anne, Brian and Desmond)

This will be the last letter I shall ever write. General weakness added to my heart failure makes it obvious that I can't last long. Madge has to do everything for me and has been and is being quite wonderful. No paid help can do the job and the invasion of privacy outweighs possible advantages – Charles and Nancy were very good and we couldn't have managed so far without them. However let's face it my time is drawing to a close rather rapidly and I don't think I'll be seeing any of you again, but don't worry about that – it's your life and your future to concentrate on.

Now may I go back to my youth. There was no surplus cash in my own family. Stress was laid on our education and the latter was aimed at making one's living in later life, which from the first was a necessity. We all had good educations – in the girls' case Flops and Mary had a year and a half at school in France (Arras) and Lausanne. Gerald became a doctor only to be killed in 1918, and Harper joined RAF on leaving Campbell at end of 1917 and then subsequent to being demobbed went to manage a sugar plantation in Zululand - he was not the academic type and joined up SA Air Force on outbreak of second world war only to be killed in an air accident while doing operational training as a gunner and wireless op. I went straight from school to university knowing full well the monetary squeeze putting one through 5 years of medical training meant to Mother and Father. I had to get through in the minimum time and just managed it. I was given £10 on graduation and not a penny thereafter.

We did not have expensive trips on holidays and no static allowance. The only trip I remember of those days was that I was allowed to go to London with Harper when he went off to South Africa to the sugar plantation – that was in 1920/1921 I think. No presents were exchanged at Christmas and we made our own fun – altogether a pretty austere upbringing, but it was not unique, as the First World War had changed the way of life of many families.

Now to move on. I met Ariel in Liverpool Stanley Hospital where we were both house surgeons in 1928. We fell in love and when a tentative offer of a job in Hong Kong was repeated in concrete form, I decided to accept and she to follow me later if I liked Hong Kong, and living there in those days was very cheap. Also Ariel was able to get a job too, so we really did well until Brian was well on the way, and again she did about 5 months work until the summer heat and Desmond decided that she should return to UK one year ahead of me – that was not uncommon in those days of no air travel.

When she died in Oct '33 – 6 weeks after Desmond was born the bottom fell out of my life. I went home pronto and had a year's leave including six months study. And managed to persuade Mary to come back to HK with Anne and the boys. She stayed 3½ years and on the whole we all had a fairly good time. Then Mary and Anne went home 1937 via USA and Mrs Deacon with Miss Hide arrived and we were very fortunate to find excellent European nanny to look after you B D and stay on at Granny's house at Waterloo when you returned to UK in May 1938 (B. D. Miss H and Granny and Monkey) I stayed on in HK moving from a big house at 288 Prince Edward Road to our apartment at 240 P E Road until I was due for leave in Feb '39 when I went home via Empress of Canada to Victoria[1] and then down through the

---

1   Where I met Madge and her husband (Herbert Molson) – I had known her at university in Edinburgh in 1924-25 and saw her several other times when, because Mrs Anderson's family lived in Victoria, I worked my trips to Europe via Vancouver / Victoria. Then she turned up in HK just as I retired in 1957.

States to August where I stayed with Alice and Harold who were holidaying there at Forest Hills Hotel and accompanied them on return to New York and so to UK on Cunard arriving late May.

The family were with Granny in Waterloo with Miss Mackay in charge and I went up to Edinburgh to do a post-graduate course in Obstetrics and Gynaecology, but the Second World War came along and the course disbanded a week early. And I was called up for RAF.

War service was varied – I had a degree in Tropical medicine, so was first MO sent to open the supply base at Takonadi in Ghana in Summer 1940 and was 3½ years in W Africa. Meantime you boys were at Holmwood, initially as commuting day boys on Southport line, but later as boarders. The last 18 months of the war saw me back in UK mostly at Bircham Newton in Norfolk where I could get the odd leave to see you. Then the war finished and I was put down for the force being formed to reoccupy Hong Kong. Brian was accepted for Marlborough and Desmond for the following year. I returned to HK in early Sept '45 and when military administration ceased there on 1st May 1946 Andy (who had been a PoW) joined me and we restarted the practice.

Such is the history. Life in HK however had changed with air travel available and I was able to get to UK for a short break every couple of years. I remember well one such break about 1954 when at the Lakes, I had a serious talk with you (B & D) and said that in 1957 I would be returning and expected you by then to have some qualifications which would enable you to support yourselves, as I would then have no income except from investment of my savings over the post-war years. You both made the deadline. I knew of course that both Aunties Flops and Mary contributed in many ways to your school and immediate post-school years. As I say life in HK had changed much from pre-war – it was more hectic and the opportunities were many.

But apart from seeing you more often in England and having you out to HK there was never any family life as such. I know you missed that, but it was just not possible if I was to make a reasonable living and save enough for retirement. I'm sorry we didn't have a family home for a least a few years but I think the way things worked out really did you good and taught you to look after yourselves with only written reference to a distant parent.

Now to get down to recent times.

Needless to say I had high hopes – probably too high – so was bound to have some disappointments and probably voiced my disappointment too forcibly and too often. Times have changed and I realise the facts of life have not. I just hope all works out well in the end.

As I sit here on my last legs let me express the pleasure it has given me to see all the third generation grow up and I do hope all will find fulfilment in life.

I love you all.
Good-bye.
Jack

When the foregoing was written I did not expect to see the month of May out as my condition was deteriorating rapidly. Then a slight adjustment of dosage in my medication – plus I <u>think</u> a decision to amend my habits and drink Spanish Champagne and beer only. Anyway something worked and I started to eat well and had no swelling of ankles – in fact feeling better but no increase in weight and strength. So I think Desmond and later Brian wondered why they had been alerted. But at the time Dr Honiton (my doctor) shared my view of rapid downhill progressing as I was not responding to any treatment. However

COLLECTING CHINA

I'm still not gaining in weight or strength although feeling better. I've not had a drop of whisky, gin or brandy since 3rd May and the last one I did have tasted so foul I poured it down the sink. Also I'm eating well and in addition taking a can of ENSURE (a whole meal so it says) per day. But as yet no increase in weight or strength – still 140-142lbs). It was grand having you (B & D) here and you now know how we are fixed help-wise. We are very reluctant to give up any of our privacy for a bit of extra help in the house and this apartment doesn't lend itself to staff living in even if such were available. For the present we can manage but if one of us becomes bed-ridden that's another matter. Liz and Maggie are very good and come over at least once a week and cook a meal for us etc. Thank goodness they live so near.

Jack died 4 April 1985.

DESCENDANTS OF REVEREND ROBERT McELNEY

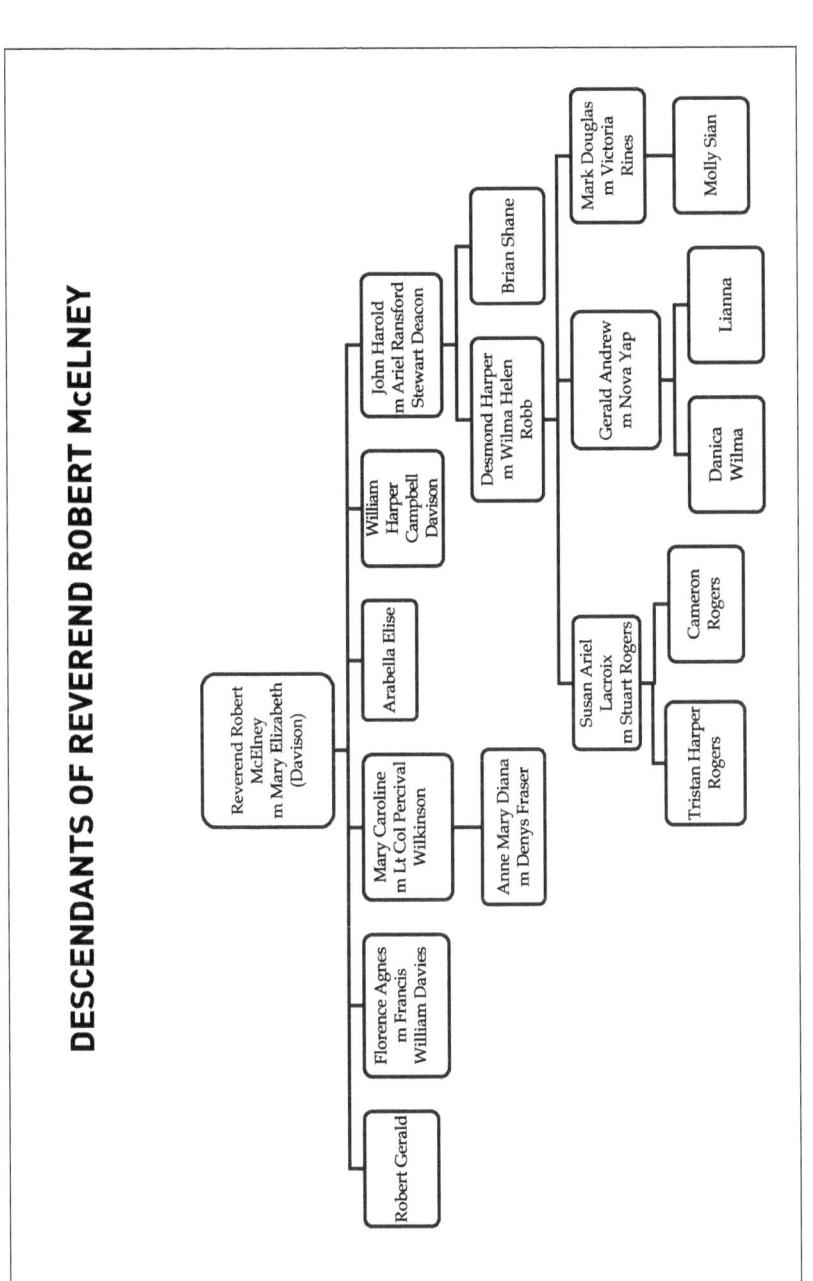

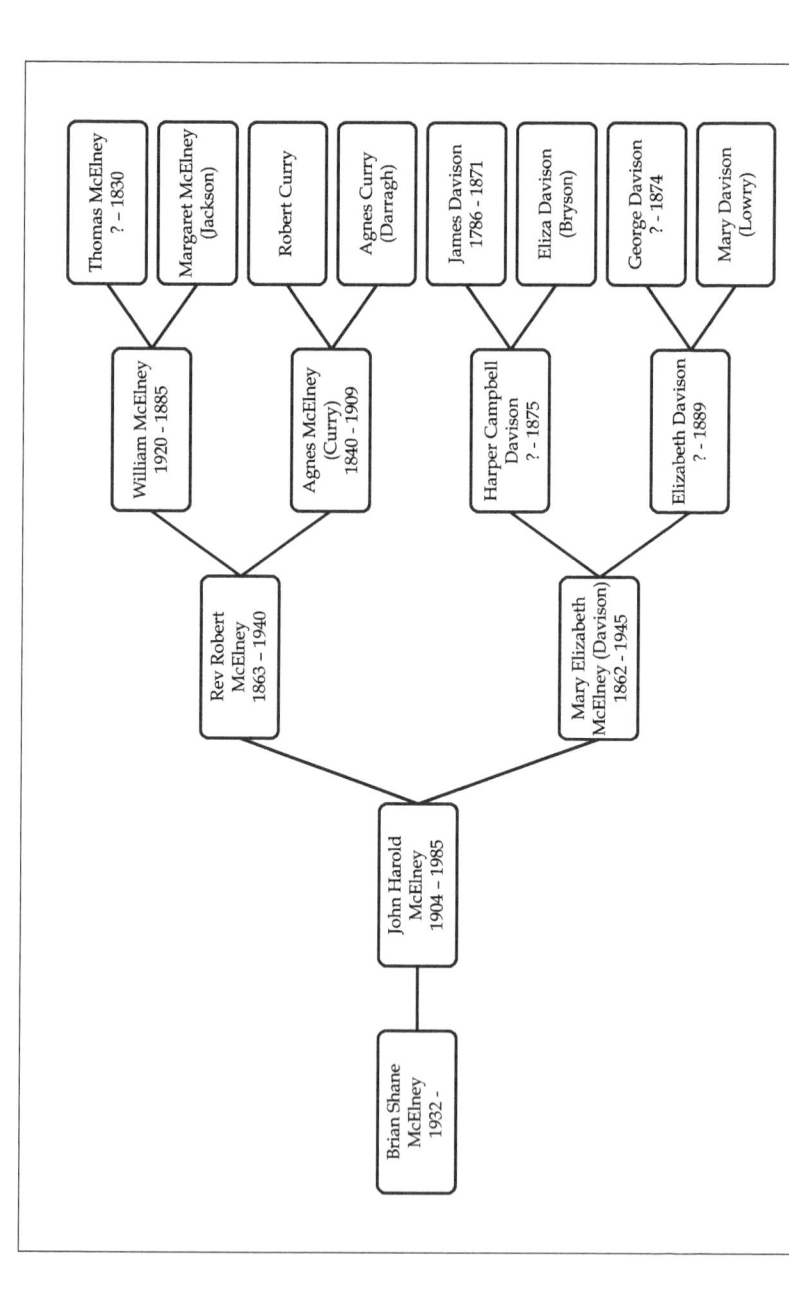

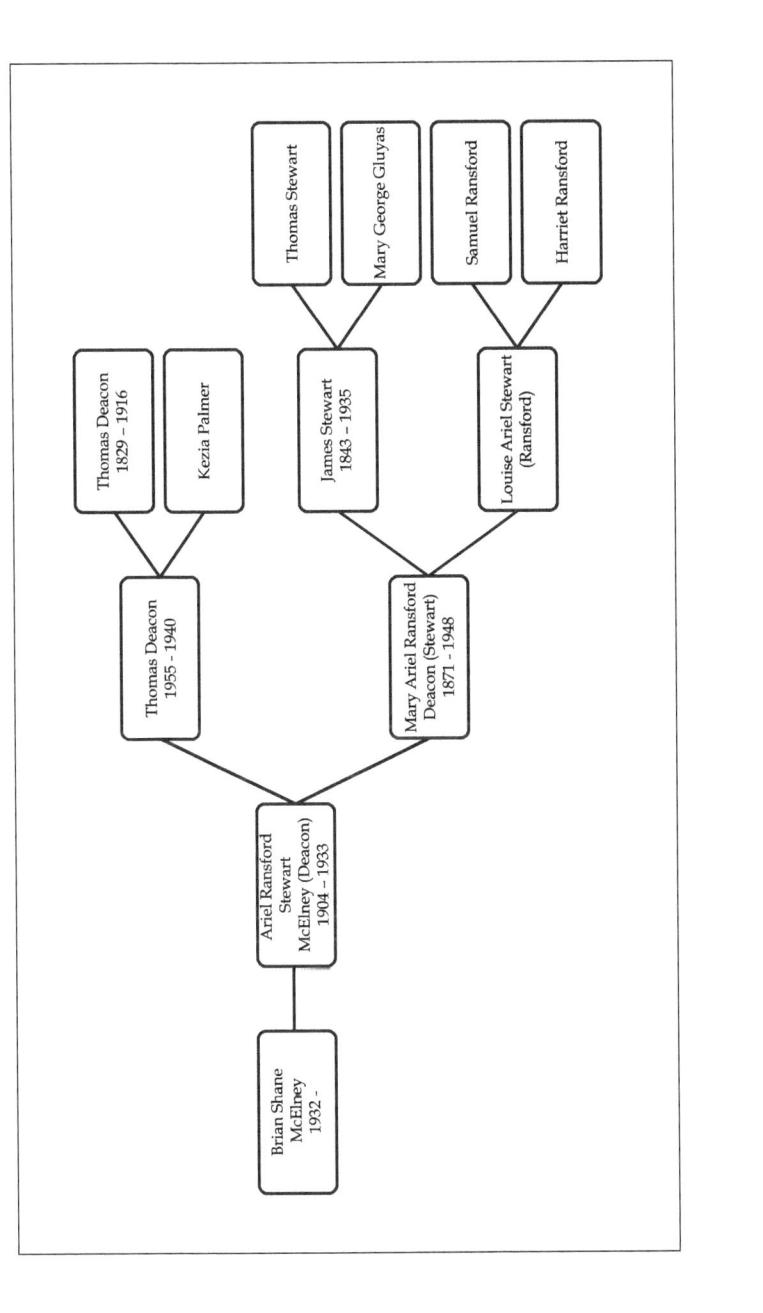

www.ingramcontent.com/pod-product-compliance
Ingram Content Group UK Ltd.
Pitfield, Milton Keynes, MK11 3LW, UK
UKHW022121230426
12048UKWH00011BA/652